Growing Up
Modern

16 QUILT PROJECTS
for Babies & Kids

Allison Harris

stashBOOKS

an imprint of C&T Publishing

Text copyright © 2013 by Allison Harris

Photography and Artwork copyright © 2013 by C&T Publishing, Inc.

PUBLISHER: Amy Marson

CREATIVE DIRECTOR: Gailen Runge

ART DIRECTOR: Kristy Zacharias

EDITOR: Liz Aneloski

TECHNICAL EDITORS: Sandy Peterson and Nanette S. Zeller

COVER/BOOK DESIGNER: April Mostek

PRODUCTION COORDINATOR: Jessica Jenkins

PRODUCTION EDITORS: S. Michele Fry and Joanna Burgarino

ILLUSTRATOR: Jenny Davis

PHOTO ASSISTANT: Cara Pardo

Styled Photography by Allison Harris

Flat Quilt Photography by Christina Carty-Francis and Diane Pedersen of C&T Publishing, Inc., unless otherwise noted

Published by Stash Books, an imprint of C&T Publishing, Inc., P.O. Box 1456, Lafayette, CA 94549

Library of Congress Cataloging-in-Publication Data

Harris, Allison, 1982-

 Growing up modern : 16 quilt projects for babies & kids / Allison Harris.

   pages cm

ISBN 978-1-60705-653-9 (soft cover)

1. Patchwork--Patterns. 2. Quilting--Patterns. 3. Children's quilts. I. Title.

TT835.H3415 2013

746.46--dc23

                    2012035171

Printed in China

10 9 8 7 6 5 4 3 2 1

Contents

Dedication and Acknowledgments 4

Preface 5

1: Making the Quilt Top 6
Tools and Supplies • Choosing Fabrics
Cutting the Fabric • Piecing

2: Finishing the Quilt 16
Making the Backing • Basting the Quilt Sandwich
Machine Quilting • Binding

3: Quilting When You Have Kids:
Finding the Time and Keeping It Fun 24

4: Projects 27–125

TUMBLE *(baby, crib, twin)* 29

BREEZY *(baby)* 35

JACK & JILL *(baby, crib, twin)* 41

BLOCKS *(baby, crib, twin)* 49

PINK HOUSES *(baby, crib, twin)* 55

STACKS *(baby)* 61

THE COLOR BLOCK QUILT *(baby)* 65

TAGGED *(baby, crib, twin)* 71

SPARKLE *(baby)* 77

SCRAPPY READER PILLOW 83

URBAN *(baby)* 87

BACK TO SCHOOL *(baby)* 93

TICK TOCK *(baby, crib, twin)* 99

QUILLOW *(crib)* 105

ROCK-A-BABY *(baby)* 113

SWEETS *(baby, crib, twin)* 119

Resources 126

About the Author 127

Dedication

This book is dedicated to my sweet family—my husband, Jay; our boys, Ben and Ryan; and our new baby, Sophie. Thank you for all the hugs, encouraging words, and take-out dinners and for being the best thing that ever happened to me.

I would also like to dedicate this book to my blog readers for all of the continued encouragement and friendship. I couldn't have done this without you.

Acknowledgments

Thank you to my parents, Trent and Dianne, for supporting this endeavor and keeping my kids entertained while I sewed. We love you tons.

A huge thank-you to C&T for this amazing opportunity and to everyone who worked so hard to make this book become a reality.

Preface

There is nothing like making a quilt for a child who will cherish it for years to come. I enjoy the quiltmaking process, but I especially love watching my kids drag their quilts around the house to be snuggled with, made into forts, and loved until the quilts are worn and thin. Whether you are making a quilt for a new baby, to tuck in a toddler, or to hang on a wall, I hope something in this book speaks to you.

The projects in this book are beginner friendly, and most of them go together very quickly. As a busy mom myself, I know time is precious, and anything too time consuming can leave you frustrated. If you are a beginner, start small and simple—*Urban* (page 87), *Stacks* (page 61), or *Tick Tock* (page 99) are good starting projects—and don't be too hard on yourself.

I encourage you to go for it. Choose a pattern, gather your supplies, and don't worry about getting it all right the first time. After all, it's a kid's quilt, and kids don't care if you make a mistake. They will love it just the same, and if all else fails, it will still make a really great fort.

Most of all, remember to enjoy the process, relax, and have fun.

—Allison

1

Making the Quilt Top

This first chapter will guide you through the basics of tools and supplies, fabric selection, cutting, and piecing the quilt top. If you feel comfortable with all of these areas, feel free to skip this next bit and refer to it as needed.

Quilt Sizes

The quilts in this book are all baby, crib, or twin size. A baby quilt is a great size for a newborn up to a toddler. A crib-size quilt is large enough for a child to snuggle on the couch or place over a toddler-sized bed. A twin-size quilt will approximately cover the twin-size mattress, but not the box spring. Before choosing which size to make, grab a measuring tape and figure out which size quilt you'd like. It's better to be sure than have a finished quilt turn out too small or too large.

Tools and Supplies

ROTARY CUTTER

Choose a rotary cutter that is 45mm or 60mm, has a retractable blade, and is comfortable to hold. Since you'll use this tool a lot, it's a good idea to buy a pack of replacement blades. My blades usually last me a handful of projects before they start to dull.

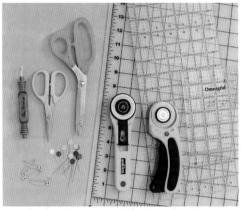

Rotary mat, ruler, rotary cutter, curved safety pins, straight pins, and fabric scissors

SELF-HEALING CUTTING MAT

Measure the amount of tabletop cutting area you have before you go shopping for a mat. I love the 24″ × 36″ size, but if you are tight on space, an 18″ × 24″ mat is fine. Make sure the mat has easy-to-see 1″ grid lines.

CUTTING RULER

There is a huge assortment of ruler sizes, but you really only need one or two. I use a 6″ × 24″ ruler for almost all my cutting. I also love the 6½″ × 6½″ ruler with a diagonal line for squaring up triangle and hourglass blocks. Whichever ruler you decide to use, make sure it's easy to see through and has easy-to-see ¼″ markings.

PINS AND SCISSORS

Pin, pin, and pin again! When it comes to quilting, you can never use too many pins, so make sure you have a lot of straight pins on hand. Curved safety pins are one of my favorite things when basting a quilt (page 18), and they can be purchased at specialty quilting or craft stores. You'll also need two pairs of sharp fabric scissors: a large pair for cutting fabric and a small pair to keep by your side for trimming threads while sewing.

SEWING MACHINE AND NEEDLES

If you don't already own a sewing machine, there are a few things to consider when buying a new one. Features you may want are feed dogs that lower, a built-in thread cutter, a needle-down position, a blanket stitch for appliqué, and a large bobbin that doesn't require as many refills. Of course, many older machines won't have all of these options, but sometimes the older machines are the best. If you are buying an older, used machine, make sure it has a good straight stitch and think about having it cleaned professionally before you use it. No matter what machine you use, make sure you have plenty of sharp needles on hand. A midsize 70/10 to 80/12 needle is good for piecing, while a larger 90/14 needle is best for machine quilting and sewing through thick fabric. Make sure you change your needle often—your machine will thank you!

THREAD

For piecing, I use 100% cotton thread. There is much debate over whether cotton or polyester is best, but I tend to stick with cotton. The high-quality threads I've tried and recommend are those by Aurifil, Mettler, Gütermann, and Superior Threads.

Choosing Fabrics

QUILTING FABRIC

Most quilting fabrics are 100% cotton and are best suited for piecing. As often as you can afford it, buy high-quality fabrics, like those from specialty quilt shops. For the backings of baby quilts, I love using soft cotton flannel or chenille fabrics. They are harder to machine quilt, but the results are soft and snuggly.

YARDAGE

A yard of fabric is 36″ long, and most quilting cotton fabric is considered 42″–45″ wide. Because the widths of fabrics vary slightly from manufacturer to manufacturer, I assume in these projects that there is only 42″ of usable width of fabric. This handy chart lists yardage increments and inches.

Yard	Inches
⅛	4½
¼	9
⅓	12
⅜	13½
½	18
⅝	22½
⅔	24
¾	27
⅞	31½
1	36

A fat quarter is half of a half-yard of fabric, or an 18″ × 22″ rectangle. It is the same amount as a quarter-yard of fabric but has more usable space. Many projects in this book use fat quarters, and I usually assume a usable area of 17½″ × 21″. Two of the projects—Stacks (page 61) and Rock-a-Baby (page 113)—need a different usable area; this is noted in their project directions.

HOW MUCH TO BUY

If you are buying fabric without any specific project in mind, a quarter- to a half-yard is usually enough. Because I like to buy a lot of different prints, I never buy more than half a yard at a time, so I can afford to purchase a variety. When I buy a yard or more, I'm almost always sick of the fabric before I get around to using it all, unless it's for a backing. In quilting, a little goes a long way, especially when you combine it with other prints.

CHOOSING PRINTS

A common question I get is how to choose fabrics and colors for a project. Although there isn't a magic answer, a few tips can help you along. I start by choosing one focal fabric, usually a large-scale print with multiple colors. I then choose a polka dot, a stripe, a small-scale fabric, and a near-solid to go with it, using the colors in my focal fabric as a guide. Don't worry if your colors don't match per-fectly; instead, focus on the hue of the fabrics and make sure the colors look pleasing together. If I need more fabrics for a project, I add more of the above, but I rarely choose

another large-scale print, because the two prints will compete for attention in the quilt and look too busy.

USING PRECUT FABRICS

If you are concerned about matching fabrics or if you like the ease of having someone choosing them all for you, precut fabrics are the way to go. Although I don't include precut-friendly patterns in this book, many patterns are available that are devoted to them. The most popular precuts are 5˝ squares, 10˝ squares, and 2½˝ strips. Most precut bundles include at least one of each print from a designer's fabric line, or about 40–42 prints.

TO PREWASH OR NOT TO PREWASH

I rarely prewash my fabrics. Prewashing removes the sizing coating that fabrics come with. High-quality fabrics are specially treated and washed to prevent bleeding, so prewashing is usually unnecessary. That being said, I do prewash cheaper-quality fabrics, as well as solid reds, blacks, and navy blues. I also pre-wash my backings if I'm using flannel, because it shrinks at a different rate than the regular quilting-weight fabrics. If you are worried about fabric bleeding, then prewash it, but most of the time you shouldn't need to. If you like the feel and crispness of new fabric, then you can always use spray starch to restore that feel when ironing after prewashing.

FABRIC TERMINOLOGY

Selvage

This is the finished edge of the fabric, which is usually printed with the names of the designer and manufacturer. Remove the finished selvages before using the fabrics, because they shrink at different rates and can distort a project.

Fold

The fold is created from folding the fabric together selvage to selvage. Make sure the selvages are aligned exactly straight so your cutting results in nice, straight strips.

Width

The width of fabric is the distance from selvage to selvage, which is most often 42″–44″.

Length

The length of fabric is the distance from the cut edge to the other cut edge. For example, if you buy a yard of fabric, the length is 36″.

Grain

The grain is the direction of the fabric's weave. In quilting cottons it runs parallel and perpendicular to the selvage (lengthwise and crosswise). Unless directed by the pattern, most cutting is done on the grain because it is less likely to stretch and distort while piecing.

Bias

The bias is the diagonal direction in relation to the grain. Fabric cut on the bias (such as triangles or circles) is more likely to stretch when piecing and should be handled carefully.

Cutting the Fabric

SQUARING UP THE FABRIC

Before you begin cutting fabric for a project, you need to square up the edge.

This is the cutting method that I use: Align the selvages parallel to the horizontal lines on the cutting mat, with the fold also parallel. Align the ruler along a vertical gridline on the cutting mat and cut off the uneven fabric edge (Figure 1). Discard the scrap. You can now begin cutting the fabric for a project.

CUTTING STRIPS AND SQUARES

If you are cutting strips, simply cut the width of strips you need using the squared-up edge as the first cut. Move the ruler down the length of the fabric, making sure the selvages are still parallel on the cutting mat (Figure 2).

If you are cutting squares, first cut the strips, and then cut the strips into squares.

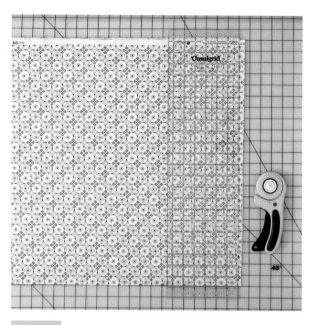

Figure 1

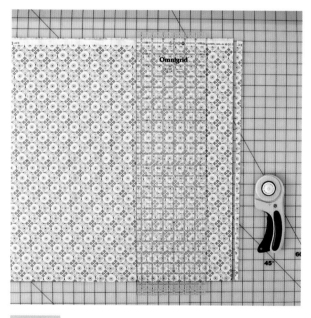

Figure 2

Piecing

THE PERFECT ¼" SEAM ALLOWANCE

When I started quilting, I *thought* I was using a ¼˝ seam allowance, but my blocks were smaller than they should have been and the pieces weren't matching perfectly. After a year of putting up with it, I realized I wasn't using an exact ¼˝ seam allowance. A lot of people assume that the foot that comes with a sewing machine is a ¼˝ foot, when in fact it's ¹⁄₁₆˝ to ⅛˝ larger than ¼˝. If you're making a block with a lot of pieces, this inaccuracy really adds up fast.

The best way to make sure you are using an accurate ¼˝ seam allowance is to use a patchwork foot made for your machine. You can always try moving your needle over to the right until you have a perfect ¼˝ allowance, but it can be hard to remember to adjust the needle every time you sit down to sew. If you're unsure how large your seam allowance is, sew a straight line with the edge of the sewing machine foot lined up with the edge of the fabric, and then measure the seam allowance with an accurate ruler.

Most projects in this book require an accurate ¼˝ seam allowance. If you find that your blocks are ending up smaller or your pieces just aren't matching up, the seam allowance could be the culprit.

CHAIN PIECING

Chain piecing means sewing pieces together one after another without stopping to cut the threads between each piece (Figure 3). After all the pieces are sewn, you can snip the threads between the pieces. Chain piecing saves huge amounts of time (and thread).

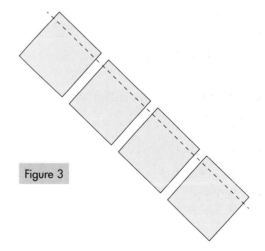

Figure 3

PRESSING

All the projects in this book require you to press well and often. Pressing refers to gently placing the iron down onto the seam and lifting it back up, instead of ironing, which refers to moving the iron around on the fabric. Pressing correctly will reduce the amount the fabric stretches and will make your piecing more accurate. If you need to press the seam to one side, gently push it open with your finger or with the edge of the iron.

In general, you usually press seams to one side and toward the darker fabric. However, sometimes I prefer to press my seams open. For example, if I have a lot of bulky seams or if my strips are very small, I would press my seams open or to the side of the smaller strip. Most of the time, it is best to press adjacent seams in alternate directions so the seams fit together. Not only will this technique create a stronger seam, but it also makes it easier to get the seams to match perfectly.

Press the Seams Out

When I give directions to "press the seams out," I mean that you should press the seams away from the center of the unit, toward the outside edges.

ADDING BORDERS

Note: For the projects in this book that include borders, specific lengths and strips will need to be cut. Use the given measurements as a guide. However, because your quilt may vary in length or width from one edge to the other, it's a good idea to measure your quilt top before adding borders.

1. If you need to piece your border strips, it is often easiest to sew all of the cut border strips together end to end, and then cut individual borders from the long strip. This makes it easy to cut 2 borders at once by folding the long strip in half, and it usually allows the seams to be in a different spot for each border.

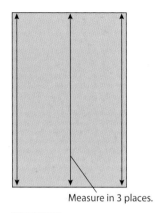

Measure in 3 places.

Figure 4

2. Place the quilt top flat on the floor and measure from top to bottom along both sides and down the center (Figure 4). Take the average of those 3 measurements. That is how long to make your side border strips. Mark the distance with a pin and cut that measurement twice from the long strip, making 2 borders.

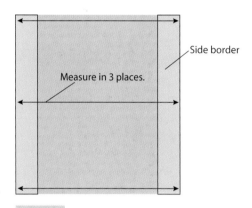

Side border

Measure in 3 places.

Figure 5

3. Pin the side borders to the side of the quilt, right sides together. Pin well, every 5″ or so. Sew the borders in place and press.

4. Repeat Steps 2 and 3 to add the top and bottom borders, except this time measure the quilt top from side to side (including the side borders) along the top, bottom, and center (Figure 5).

2
Finishing the Quilt

This chapter covers the basics of backings, battings, making a quilt sandwich, machine quilting, and binding. If you're like most people, making the quilt top is the fun part, but finishing it is where you're likely to get stuck. I hope this bit of the book will help you get your quilt tops finished and put to good use!

Making the Backing

Making the quilt backing is super simple. Using the required yardage, cut the fabric into two equal lengths, trim off the selvages, and sew the trimmed selvage edges right sides together. Press the entire backing, and you're good to go. Making a pieced back is a great way to use up large leftover pieces of fabrics. Simply piece the backing as desired until it is large enough.

The projects in this book are relatively small, so I usually use simple quilting designs that are not dense. That being said, if you are quilting the quilt yourself, an extra 2″ of backing material around all the edges of your quilt top is adequate. If you are having it quilted by a longarm quilter, check with the quilter to see how much extra is needed around each edge (usually 4″–6″). Thus, if you want to have your quilt longarm quilted, you may need to purchase additional backing fabric.

Batting

I personally prefer thin cotton batting in all of my quilts. It's warm and easy to work with, and I like the look of it when it shrinks up after washing. My favorite type is Warm & White from The Warm Company, especially for quilts with a lot of white or light fabrics in them. With  so many different options to choose from, try a few until you find a batting you love. I also use an extra 2″ of batting all around my quilt top.

Basting the Quilt Sandwich

Basting can either make or break your finished quilt, but it's easy to do once you know how. There are a couple of ways to baste a quilt, but this is the method I prefer:

1. Lay your quilt backing flat on a clean floor, right side down. Using masking tape, tape the corners and sides of the quilt backing until it's taut, but not stretched.

2. Place the batting on top of the backing, smoothing out any wrinkles with your hands.

3. Place the quilt top on the batting, right side up, making sure the top is centered and there is at least 2″ of batting and backing all around the quilt top. Smooth the quilt with your hands.

4. With safety pins (curved safety pins are my favorite), pin through the 3 layers every 6″ or so.

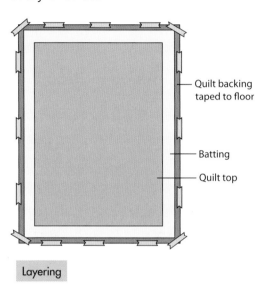

Quilt backing taped to floor

Batting

Quilt top

Layering

BASTING SPRAY

If the thought of pinning every 6″ makes you cringe, you may want to give basting spray a try. Instead of pinning, the layers can be sprayed lightly to make them tacky, then smoothed out just like you normally would. I prefer not using basting spray because of the strong smell and the sticky mess, but I know quilters who swear by it and use nothing else.

Machine Quilting

Machine quilting scares a lot of new quilters, but it is easy (and fun!) once you get the hang of it. Keep in mind that you won't get it right the first time, or even the fifth time, but after awhile, it will become more comfortable, and your quilting will improve.

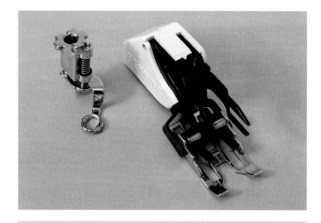

Darning or free-motion quilting foot and a walking foot for machine quilting

FREE-MOTION QUILTING

To free-motion quilt, you will need a free-motion, or darning, foot for your machine. Once the foot is on, lower the feed dogs and set the stitch length as low as it can go. Start at the quilt's top right corner, or at one of the top edges, and move the quilt under the foot as you press the pedal down about three-quarters of the way. Free-motion quilting is similar to drawing, so think of your needle as the pencil as you draw the design onto the quilt, filling in the spaces until you are done.

My favorite free-motion design is called stippling, but you can also have fun making loops, circles, or any other design you can think of. It takes a lot of practice to get it right, and it may never be perfect, but once you get the hang of it, free-motion quilting is really fun to do!

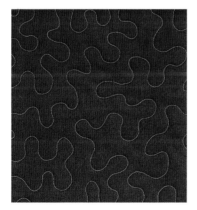  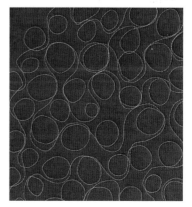

Stippling, loopy quilting, and circles

STRAIGHT-LINE QUILTING

To straight-line quilt, you need a walking foot for your machine. Try quilting with random straight lines, or follow the quilt design ¼″ away from the seams. If you need help making a straight line on the quilt top, place masking tape in a straight line across the quilt and follow the edge of the tape with the edge of your walking foot. You can then take the tape off and use the previous stitched line as a guide.

LONGARM QUILTING

Machine quilting can be tricky to do on large quilts, which is why I love longarm quilters. A professional quilter will load your backing, batting, and top onto the quilting frame and move the machine over the quilt to make the design. I take any quilt tops twin-sized and larger to a longarm quilter. Although it does cost more, it saves my back hours of maneuvering a large quilt through my small machine.

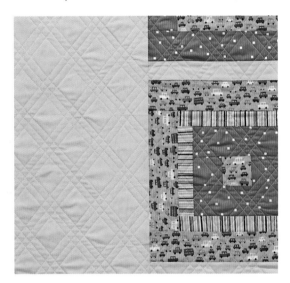

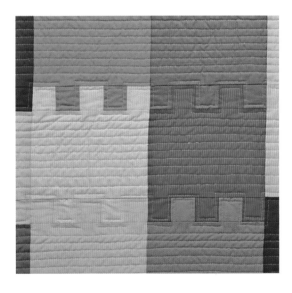

Photo by Allison Harris

Binding

I use a double-fold binding for all of my quilts. The most popular method of binding is to sew the binding to the front of the quilt by machine, and then hand sew it to the back. However, since most of the quilts I make are heavily used by my kids or given as baby gifts, I prefer machine stitching the binding to the back instead. That way, when I give a quilt as a gift or make one for my own boys, I don't have to worry when it's thrown into the washing machine twenty times. On special quilts or quilts I make just for me, however, I enjoy hand sewing the binding, because it definitely has a nicer finished look.

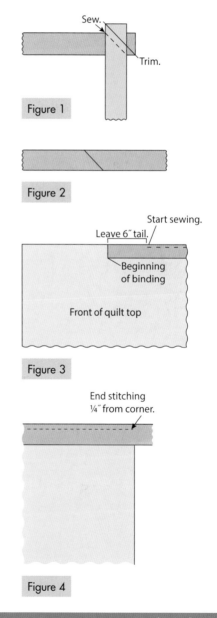

Figure 1

Figure 2

Figure 3

Figure 4

PREPARE THE BINDING

1. Cut the required number of 2½˝ strips for the quilt you are binding and trim off the selvages. Sew the strips together by laying one strip over the end of another strip, right sides together at 90°. Mark a diagonal line, pin, and sew on the line (Figure 1).

2. Trim off the corner, leaving a ¼˝ seam allowance, and press the seam open. Continue until all of the binding strips are sewn together.

3. Press the long binding strip in half lengthwise with wrong sides together, so that both raw edges are on one edge and the fold is on the other. The binding strip is now 1¼˝ wide (Figure 2).

ATTACH THE BINDING

1. Start on a side of the quilt, leaving 6˝ of extra binding at the beginning. Align the raw edges of the binding strip with the raw edges of the quilt. Use a ¼˝ seam allowance to sew the binding strip to the quilt (Figure 3). Use a walking foot if you have one.

2. Sew until you are ¼˝ from a corner. Backstitch and remove the quilt from under the presser foot (Figure 4).

Fold up the binding strip so its raw edges are in line with the next side of the quilt, creating a 45° fold (Figure 5).

3. Pin or hold the 45° fold as you place the remaining binding strip back down over the fold, so the edges are aligned with the next side of the quilt. This creates another fold at the top edge of the quilt (Figure 6). Start sewing at the top of that fold and continue until you are ¼˝ from the next corner. Repeat Steps 2 and 3 for each corner.

4. Stop stitching 6˝ from where you began binding the quilt; backstitch. Remove the quilt from under the presser foot, fold the end of the binding back where it meets the beginning binding tail, and press enough to make a visible crease. From that fold, measure 2½˝ along the ending binding tail and cut (Figure 7). Open both binding tails and place one on top of the other, right sides together, at right angles, as you did when you first sewed the binding strips together. Mark a diagonal line, stitch along the line, and trim the corner, leaving a ¼˝ seam allowance (Figure 8). Press open. Refold and press the binding. Then stitch the last bit to the quilt.

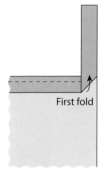

First fold

Figure 5

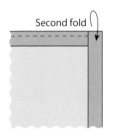

Second fold

Figure 6

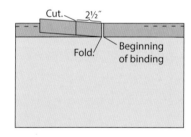

Cut. 2½˝

Fold.

Beginning of binding

Figure 7

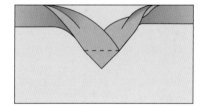

Figure 8

5. To hand sew the binding to the back of the quilt, fold the binding from the front of the quilt to the back, miter the corners, and hand sew into place.

To machine sew the binding to the back of the quilt, fold the binding from the front of the quilt to the back and miter the corners as you normally would. Pin the binding to the back, extending the fold of the binding strip *just barely* beyond the ¼˝ stitch line that you created when sewing the binding to the front of the quilt. Using a walking foot, start sewing the binding to the back of the quilt as closely as you can get to the edge of the binding fold. When you get to a corner, simply miter and sew the corner down, just as you would if you were hand stitching, keeping the needle down in the corner when you rotate the quilt under the presser foot.

The machine binding stitches will be visible on the front of the quilt, but if you extend the fold of the binding strip just past the ¼˝ stitch line on the back of the quilt, then the binding on the front of the quilt should have no stitches in it, just as a hand sewn binding would. This takes some practice, but it's worth learning to do!

Binding hand sewn to back

Binding that is machine sewn to the back

3
Quilting When You Have Kids:
Finding the Time and Keeping It Fun

Free time is hard to come by these days—especially when you're raising little kids. Here are a few tips that might make it easier to fit a little quilting into your day.

Quilt in Small Bursts

There's probably no way you're going to find an extra hour or two in your day to make a quilt. But you may find ten minutes, six times a day when you can sit down and cut your fabric or sew a block. You'll be surprised how fast you can complete a whole quilt by taking advantage of small bits of time here and there. I rarely have a whole hour to sit and sew, but I can get a lot done if I sneak over to my sewing machine a few times a day for ten to twenty minutes at a time—or until my kids find me.

Be Realistic

Starting small and simple is the best advice I got when I started quilting, and it still holds true. Be realistic about how much time, money, and effort you can afford to put into quilting and start there. If you can only spare ten minutes a day and $30 worth of fabric, making a king-size quilt just doesn't make sense. You're more likely to finish and feel good about the process if you start with a baby or crib quilt that you can finish quickly.

Don't Get Sidetracked

I used to be the queen of unfinished projects. I would get inspired and start a project, only to be inspired and start a different project the next day, and so on, and so on. It made sewing stressful. Now I choose two projects at a time to focus on. One is a short-term project, such as a baby quilt or pillow cover; the other is a larger, long-term project, such as a twin-size quilt that I work on a little at a time.

Involve Your Kids

I know letting your kids "help" sounds like the opposite of finding time, but they love being a part of what you are doing, And let's face it—they will be at your side whether or not you want them to be. Here are a few things my kids enjoy doing while I sew:

■ **Making scrap art**

Cut extra scraps into small bits or save small fabric pieces you would normally throw in the trash. Cut out a shape or letter from cardboard or cardstock, and let your child glue or tape the scraps to it until it's completely covered.

■ Sorting colors

My kids will take any chance they can get to play in my basket of fabric scraps. To keep them from making a mess, I ask them to sort the scraps into color piles. Even my two-year-old enjoys putting the blue scraps in the blue pile and so on until all of the scraps are gone. When they are done, if they put all of the scraps back into the basket, they get to choose one scrap to keep.

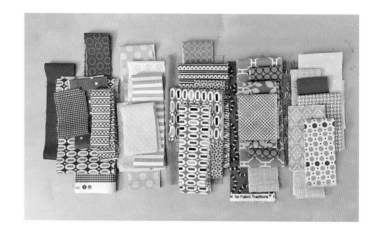

■ Letting them help

My five-year-old loves to help me in my sewing room, and now that he's older, there are some extra things he can help me do. I let him put fabrics away after I'm done cutting, put scraps in the scrap basket or trash, put pins and safety pins back into the pincushions, clip threads between blocks while I chain piece (with his safety scissors), and help me smooth out the quilt layers when I'm making the quilt sandwich.

As always, use good judgment when it comes to letting your children help, and keep any sharp tools away from curious little hands.

4

Projects

28 **34** **40** **48** **54**

60 **64** **70** **76** **82**

86 **92** **98** **104** **112** **118**

Tumble

Pieced by Allison Harris and quilted by Lindsay Szechenyi

Whether you're making a quilt for a sweet newborn, a busy toddler, or a too-cool teenager, Tumble *is perfect for any age. The stack-and-cut assembly technique makes it a perfect first quilt for beginners.*

FINISHED BLOCK: 5½″ × 7″

FINISHED QUILT

BABY: 33½″ × 42½″ • CRIB: 44½″ × 49½″ • TWIN: 66½″ × 91½″

Quilt shown in a crib size

Yardage is based on 42″-wide fabric. In some cases, you might have a few extra cut pieces.

Size	Fabric	Yardage	Cutting	Subcut
Baby	Prints	6 regular or fat quarters	6 squares 7″ × 7″ from each fabric* (36 total)	
	Neutral	½ yard	6 strips 2″ × fabric width	36 strips 2″ × 6″
	Backing	1½ yards		
	Binding	½ yard	5 strips 2½″ × fabric width	
	Batting	38″ × 47″		
Crib	Prints	10 regular or fat quarters	6 squares 7″ × 7″ from each fabric* (56 total)	
	Neutral	½ yard	8 strips 2″ × fabric width	56 strips 2″ × 6″
	Backing	2⅞ yards		
	Binding	½ yard	6 strips 2½″ × fabric width	
	Batting	49″ × 54″		
Twin	Prints	26 regular or fat quarters	6 squares 7″ × 7″ from each fabric* (156 total)	
	Neutral	1⅓ yards	23 strips 2″ × fabric width	156 strips 2″ × 6″
	Backing	5½ yards		
	Binding	¾ yard	9 strips 2½″ × fabric width	
	Batting	71″ × 96″		

* See Fat quarter cutting (page 31)

Tip

These quilt blocks are easy to make larger or smaller. Start with a larger or smaller print square, and use the same cutting and sewing technique. Then, cut and add a neutral strip that is the same width as your finished square.

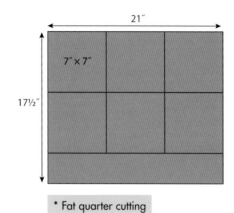

21″

7″ × 7″

17½″

* Fat quarter cutting

Block Assembly

Note that all sewing is done right sides together with a ¼″ seam allowance.

1. Stack 2 coordinating print 7″ × 7″ squares (Figure 1).

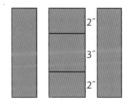

Figure 1

2. Make a vertical cut 2″ in from each side (Figure 2).

3. Make a horizontal cut 2″ in from the top and bottom edges of the 3″ × 7″ center strip (Figure 3).

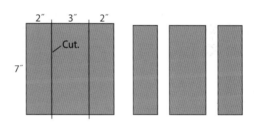

2″   3″   2″

Cut.

7″

Figure 2

2″

3″

2″

Figure 3

4. You now have 2 strips 2″ × 7″, 2 strips 2″ × 3″, and 1 square 3″ × 3″ of *each* print (Figure 4).

5. Swap the center 3″ × 3″ square with the other coordinating 3″ × 3″ square.

6. Sew the 2″ × 3″ strips back onto the top and bottom edges of each 3″ × 3″ square. Press the seams out (Figure 5).

7. Sew the 2″ × 7″ strips to each side of the center strip (Figure 6). Don't worry about the overhang, because you'll square-up the blocks next. Press the seams out.

8. Square-up the top and bottom edges by aligning your ruler with the top of the center section and cutting off the overhang (Figure 7). The units measure 6″ × 6″.

9. Sew a neutral 2″ × 6″ strip onto the bottom edge of each unit from Step 8 (Figure 8). Press the seams toward the center if you are using a light neutral or toward the neutral strip if the neutral fabric is dark. The unfinished block measures 6″ × 7½″.

10. Make the following:

36 blocks for the baby size

56 blocks for the crib size

156 blocks for the twin size

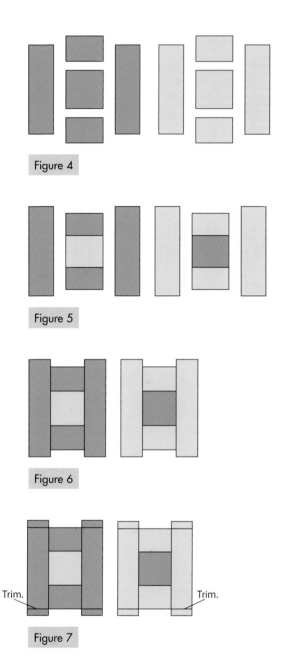

Figure 4

Figure 5

Figure 6

Trim.   Trim.

Figure 7

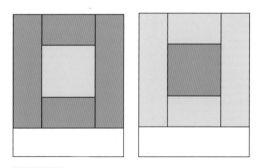

Figure 8

Quilt Top Assembly

1. Lay out the blocks as follows (Figure 9):

6 rows of 6 blocks for the baby size

7 rows of 8 blocks for the crib size

13 rows of 12 blocks for the twin size

Rotate the blocks in a row so the neutral strips face down, then up, and so on. Continue with each row, rotating the same blocks for each row.

2. Sew the blocks into rows and press the seams in alternate directions.

3. Sew the rows together and press well to finish the quilt top.

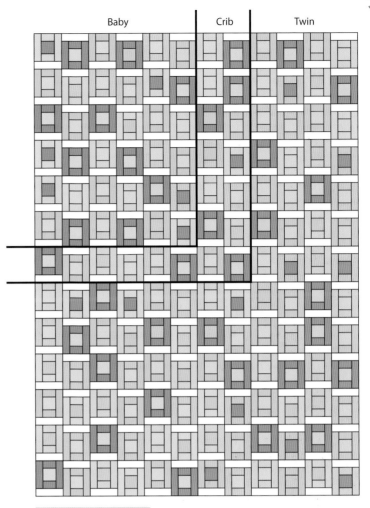

Baby   Crib   Twin

Figure 9—Quilt layout

Finishing

Refer to Finishing the Quilt (pages 16–23) for information on making the backing, quilting, and binding the quilt.

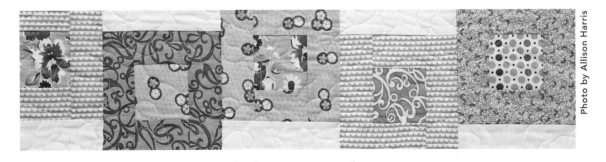

Photo by Allison Harris

Tumble

Breezy

Pieced and quilted by Allison Harris

Simple strips make this quilt a breeze to put together. Use the simple yardage requirements given, or use precut 2½″ strips.

FINISHED BLOCK: 8″ × 6″

FINISHED BABY QUILT:

40½″ × 47½″

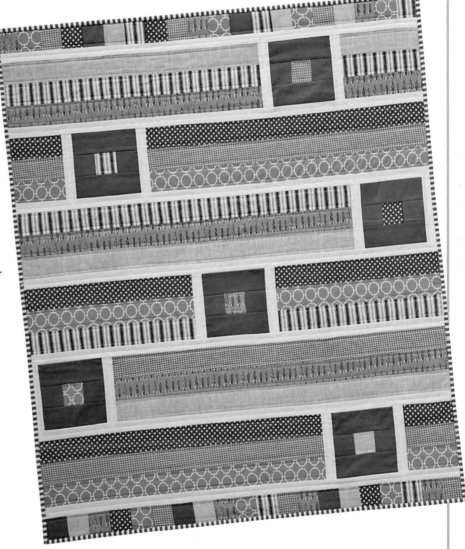

Yardage is based on 42″-wide fabric unless noted.

Fabric	Yardage	Cutting	Subcut
Prints	⅜ yard each of 6 fabrics	3 strips 2½″ × fabric width from each fabric (18 total)	1 strip 2½″ × 33″ and 3 squares 2½″ × 2½″ from each fabric strip
Solid	⅜ yard	3 strips 2½″ × fabric width	4 strips 2½″ × 6½″ and 6 squares 2½″ × 2½″ from each fabric strip
White	½ yard	2 strips 1½″ × fabric width	12 strips 1½″ × 6½″
		7 strips 1½″ × fabric width	7 strips 1½″ × 40½″
Backing	1⅝ yards*; OR 2⅝ yards**		
Binding	½ yard	5 strips 2½″ × fabric width	
Batting	45″ × 52″		

* If the fabric is 45″ wide and you use 2″ extra on each side of the quilt top

** If the fabric is 42″ wide and you use 2″ extra on each side of the quilt top

Block Assembly

Note that all sewing is done right sides together with a ¼″ seam allowance.

1. Choose a print 2½″ × 2½″ square. Pin and sew a solid 2½″ × 2½″ square to each side of the print square. Press the seams out. Pin and sew a solid 2½″ × 6½″ strip to the top and bottom of the unit. Press out. The unit measures 6½″ × 6½″. Pin and sew a white 1½″ × 6½″ strip to each side of the unit. Press the seams out (Figure 1). The block measures 8½″ × 6½″.

2. Repeat Step 1 to make 6 blocks, using a different 2½″ × 2½″ print square for the center of each block.

Quilt Top Assembly

1. Lay out the 2½″ × 33″ print strips in the order you want them for the quilt top. Pin and sew the strips together into 6 sets of 3 strips each. Press the seams open or to either side (Figure 2).

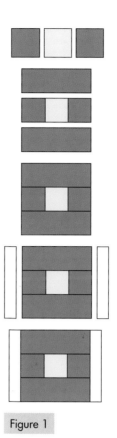

Figure 1

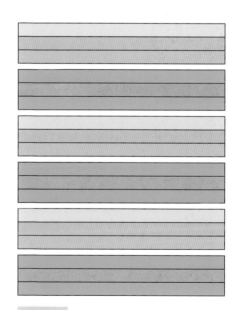

Figure 2

2. Measure and cut 4 of the 6 strip sets as follows, using Figure 3 for reference. Make sure not to cut the third or fifth strip set.

Strip set 1: Make a cut 8˝ from the right side.

Strip set 2: Make a cut 5½˝ from the left side.

Strip set 3: Don't cut.

Strip set 4: Make a cut in the center, or 16½˝ in from either edge.

Strip set 5: Don't cut.

Strip set 6: Make a cut 5½˝ from the right side.

3. Pin and sew a block between each of the cut pieces on each strip set (Figure 4).

4. Sew a block to the right edge of the third strip set. Sew a block to the left edge of the fifth strip set. On both the third and fifth strip sets, trim ½˝ from the short edge opposite the blocks, making both strip sets with blocks 40½˝ long.

5. All 6 of the strip sets with blocks measure 6½˝ × 40½˝.

6. Place a white 1½˝ × 40½˝ strip between each strip set from Step 5 and at the top of the first and bottom of the last strip sets. Pin and sew the white strips and the strip sets together. Press the seams open or toward the print strips.

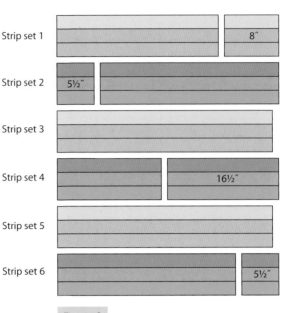

Figure 3

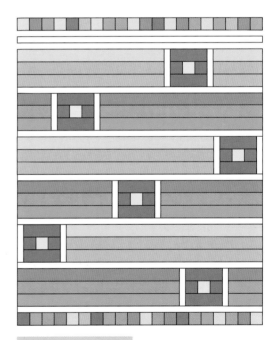

Figure 4—Quilt layout

7. Make the top and bottom border by laying out 2 rows of 20 leftover 2½˝ × 2½˝ squares (you will have extra for color arrangement). Pin and sew the squares together and press the seams in the same direction or open. Each border measures 2½˝ × 40½˝.

8. Sew the top and bottom borders to the quilt top and press the seams open or toward the borders.

Finishing

Refer to Finishing the Quilt (pages 16–23) for information on making the backing, quilting, and binding the quilt.

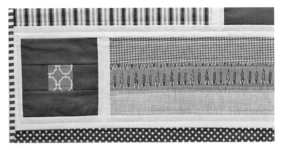

Jack & Jill

Pieced by Allison Harris and
quilted by Christina Lane

Scrappy, raw-edge circles are my favorite, especially when they are this easy to make! This quilt is easy enough for a beginner, and the raw edges give it lots of texture. Using spray starch and pins instead of fusible web will leave the quilt soft and cuddly after washing.

Quilt shown in a crib size

FINISHED BLOCK: 7½″ × 7½″

FINISHED QUILT • **BABY:** 38″ × 50″ • **CRIB:** 45½″ × 57½″ • **TWIN:** 68″ × 87½″

Yardage is based on 42˝-wide fabric. In some cases, you might have a few extra cut pieces.

Size	Fabric	Yardage	Cutting	Subcut
Baby	Prints	5 fat quarters or ⅜ yard of 5 fabrics*	5 squares 7˝ × 7˝ (25 total) and 6 rectangles 3˝ × 5˝ (30 total) from each fabric**	
	Background solid	1⅞ yards	7 strips 8½˝ × fabric width	25 squares 8½˝ × 8½˝
	Inner border	¼ yard	2 strips 2˝ × fabric width	
	Backing	1⅝ yards		
	Binding	½ yard	5 strips 2½˝ × fabric width	
	Batting	42˝ × 54˝		
Crib	Prints	8 fat quarters or ⅜ yard of 8 fabrics*	5 squares 7˝ × 7˝ (36 total) and 5 rectangles 3˝ × 5˝ (36 total) from each fabric**	
	Background solid	2¼ yards	9 strips 8½˝ × fabric width	36 squares 8½˝ × 8½˝
	Inner border	¼ yard	3 strips 2˝ × fabric width	
	Backing	3 yards		
	Binding	½ yard	6 strips 2½˝ × fabric width	
	Batting	50˝ × 62˝		

Size	Fabric	Yardage	Cutting	Subcut
Twin	Prints	18 fat quarters or ⅜ yard of 18 fabrics*	5 squares 7″ × 7″ (90 total) and 3 rectangles 3″ × 5″ (54 total) from each fabric**	
	Background solid	5⅝ yards	23 strips 8½″ × fabric width	90 squares 8½″ × 8½″
	Inner border	⅓ yard	4 strips 2″ × fabric width	
	Backing	5¼ yards		
	Binding	¾ yard	9 strips 2½″ × fabric width	
	Batting	72″ × 92″		

* Add additional fabrics for a scrappier look and more variety in fabric placement.

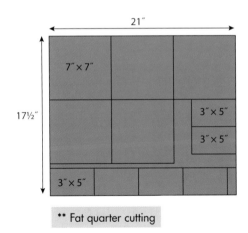

** Fat quarter cutting

ADDITIONAL MATERIALS
Spray starch

Block Assembly

Note that all sewing is done right sides together with a ¼″ seam allowance.

1. Starch the background solid (I used white) 8½″ × 8½″ squares and the print 7″ × 7″ squares until the fabrics are slightly stiff and paper-like. Be careful not to stretch the fabric when pressing.

2. Trace the circle pattern (page 47) onto paper and cut it out.

3. Pin the circle template onto the back of each 7″ × 7″ print square *or* use a pencil to trace the circle onto the backs of the squares. Cut around the circles with scissors.

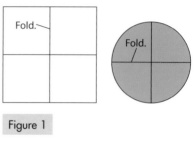

Figure 1

Tip

Stack, pin, and cut two or more circles at a time to speed up the cutting.

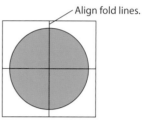

Figure 2

4. Choose a white 8½″ × 8½″ square and a print 7″ circle to make a block (Figure 1).

5. Gently fold each piece in half both ways, finger pressing the fold lines along the edges. Place the print circle right side up on the white square, aligning the fold lines to center the circle (Figure 2). Pin well.

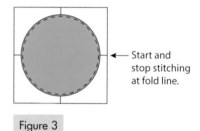

Figure 3

6. Starting and ending on one of the half-folds, sew ¼″ in from the edge of the circle, leaving the edges raw (Figure 3). Backstitch at the beginning and end.

NOTE *If the fabric is bunching or pulling as you stitch around the circle, keep the needle down as you lift the presser foot and adjust the fabric slightly so you can continue around the circle. Lower the presser foot and stitch. You may also need to use more starch to keep the bias edges from stretching.*

7. Make the following:

25 blocks for the baby size

36 blocks for the crib size

90 blocks for the twin size

8. Align each block on the cutting mat, and cut each block in half both ways, 4¼˝ from the sides (Figure 4). Each block is divided into 4 squares 4¼˝ × 4¼˝.

9. Using scissors, cut away the white fabric from behind each print quarter-circle, leaving a ¼˝ seam allowance (Figure 5). This step takes time but will reduce bulk and make it easier to sew the blocks together.

10. Mix the 4¼˝ × 4¼˝ squares and choose 4 different fabrics to make a block (Figure 6). Match the seams as best as possible, pin, and sew them together to form a circle. Press the seams open to reduce bulk. Don't worry about aligning the circle seams perfectly—after washing, the edges will fray, and misalignments won't be noticeable. The unfinished blocks measure 8˝ × 8˝.

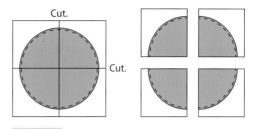

Cut.

Cut.

Figure 4

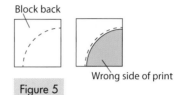

Block back

Wrong side of print

Figure 5

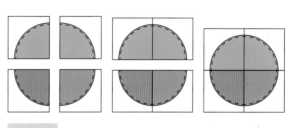

Figure 6

Quilt Top Assembly

1. Lay out the blocks (Figure 7):

5 rows of 5 blocks for the baby size

6 rows of 6 blocks for the crib size

10 rows of 9 blocks for the twin size

2. Sew the blocks into rows and press, alternating pressing directions in each row.

3. Sew the rows together to make the quilt center; press.

4. Refer to Adding Borders (page 14) to measure, construct, and cut the inner border strips. For the crib and twin size, sew the border strips together end to end to make a long strip. Cut to length. Pin and sew a border strip onto the top of the quilt top and sew the remaining strip onto the bottom. Press the seams out.

5. Make the outer borders by sewing together the 3″ × 5″ print strips along the 5″ sides. Press the seams open. For the baby size, you need 2 borders that are 15 strips wide. For the crib size, you need 2 borders that are 18 strips wide. For the twin size, you need 2 borders that are 27 strips wide.

6. Pin the borders to the top and bottom of the quilt, sew, and press the seams in to finish the quilt top.

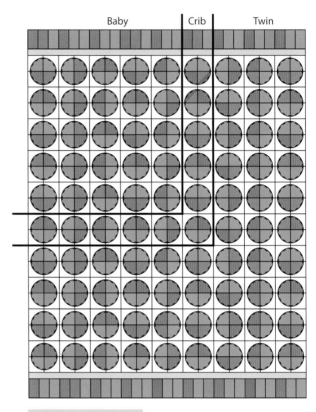

Figure 7—Quilt layout

Note: Include inner and outer borders at the top and bottom of all sizes of quilts.

Finishing

Refer to Finishing the Quilt (pages 16–23) for information on making the backing, quilting, and binding the quilt.

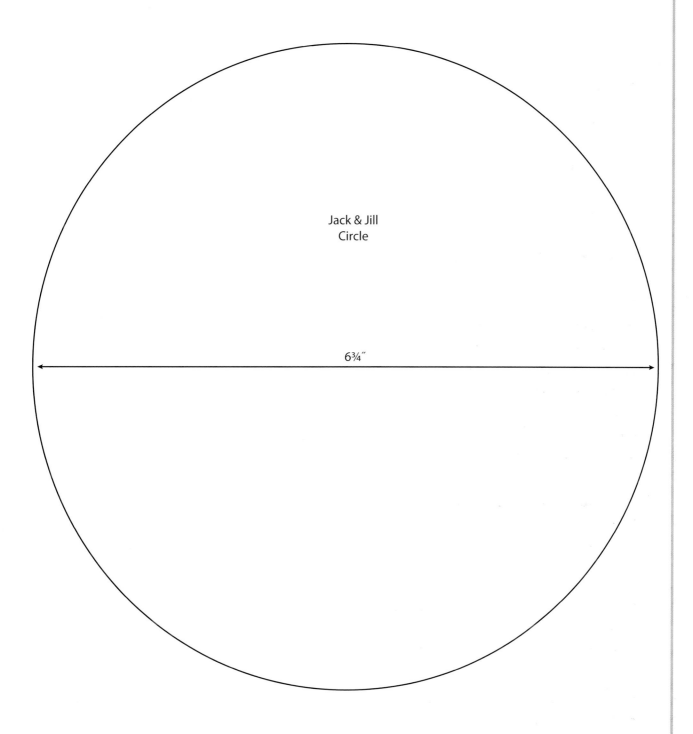

Jack & Jill
Circle

6¾″

Blocks

Pieced and quilted by Allison Harris

I made this quilt for my block-loving boys. It's simple, bright, and a lot quicker to clean up than blocks all over my floor. If you keep a close eye on the layout diagram, you should have this quilt made in no time. Try using small prints instead of solids for more variety.

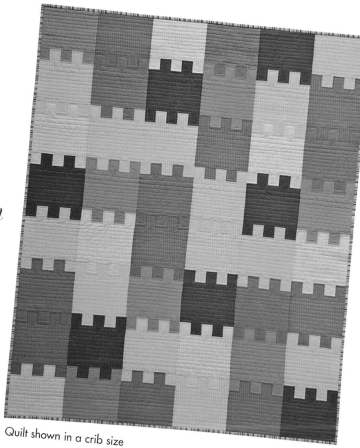

Quilt shown in a crib size

FINISHED QUILT

BABY: 38″ × 48″ • CRIB: 45½″ × 55″ • TWIN: 68″ × 90″

Yardage is based on 42˝-wide fabric. In some cases, you might have a few extra cut pieces.

Size	Fabric	Yardage	Cutting	Subcut
Baby	Solids	⅜ yard each of 5 fabrics	1 strip 8˝ × fabric width from each fabric	7 rectangles 6˝ × 8˝ from each strip (35 total)
			2 strips 2˝ × fabric width from each fabric	35 squares 2˝ × 2˝ from each strip pair
	Backing	1⅝ yards		
	Binding	½ yard	5 strips 2½˝ × fabric width	
	Batting	42˝ × 52˝		
Crib	Solids	⅜ yard each of 7 fabrics	1 strip 8˝ × fabric width from each fabric	7 rectangles 6˝ × 8˝ from each strip (48 total)
			2 strips 2˝ × fabric width from each fabric	35 squares 2˝ × 2˝ from each strip pair
	Backing	3 yards		
	Binding	½ yard	6 strips 2½˝ × fabric width	
	Batting	50˝ × 59˝		

Size	Fabric	Yardage	Cutting	Subcut
Twin	Solids	⅜ yard each of 17 fabrics	1 strip 8″ × fabric width from each fabric	7 rectangles 6″ × 8″ from each 8″ strip (117 total)
			2 strips 2″ × fabric width from each fabric	35 squares 2″ × 2″ from each strip pair
	Backing	5⅜ yards		
	Binding	¾ yard	9 strips 2½″ × fabric width	
	Batting	72″ × 94″		

Quilt Assembly

Note that all sewing is done right sides together with a ¼″ seam allowance.

This quilt is simple, but it can get a little confusing once you start laying out all of the pieces. Make sure you have enough space to lay out the quilt pieces and leave them there as you sew the top together.

1. Refer to the quilt layout diagram (page 52) as you lay out the 6″ × 8″ rectangles, arranging the colors as desired and leaving enough space between the rectangles to place the 2″ × 2″ squares.

5 *columns* of 7 blocks for the baby size

6 *columns* of 8 blocks for the crib size

9 *columns* of 13 blocks for the twin size

2. Starting with the first block of the first column, lay out 3 of the same color 2″ × 2″ squares below this block. Between those 3 squares, place 2 squares that match the second block in the column. Continue down Column 1 until you've placed squares between each block.

3. Sew the first column together by sewing together the 5 small squares from Step 2; press the seams open and then sew the blocks and squares together to form the column. Press all the seams down toward the bottom of the column.

4. Starting with the first block in Column 2, lay out 2 matching squares below it, instead of 3 squares as you did with Column 1. Between those 2 squares, place 3 squares that match the second block in the column. Continue down Column 2 until you've placed squares between each block.

5. Sew the second column together as in Step 3 and press all the seams up toward the top of the column.

6. Lay out Column 3 as you did Column 1. Lay out Column 4 as you did Column 2, and so on, alternating between having 3 or 2 matching 2″ × 2″ squares below the blocks of the columns.

7. Sew each of the blocks and squares into columns, as explained in Steps 3 and 5, and press.

8. Match and pin the seams, sew the columns together, and press the seams in the same direction to finish the quilt top.

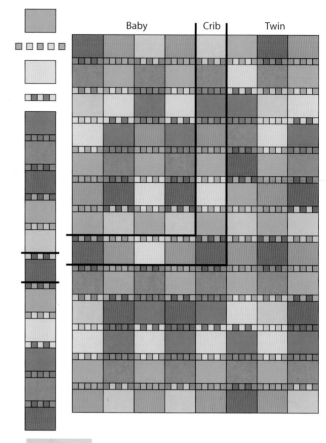

Quilt layout

Finishing

Refer to Finishing the Quilt (pages 16–23) for information on making the backing, quilting, and binding the quilt.

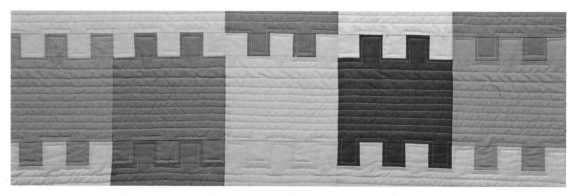

Pink Houses

Pieced by Allison Harris and quilted by Christina Lane

Little pink houses all in a row make up this sweet quilt. Quick piecing shortcuts make it easy to put together. For the best results, use a combination of small-scale prints and near-solids.

FINISHED BLOCK: 6″ × 9½″

FINISHED QUILT • **BABY:** 36½″ × 48″

CRIB: 48½″ × 57½″ • **TWIN:** 66½″ × 86″

Quilt shown in a crib size

Yardage is based on 42˝-wide fabric. In some cases, you might have a few extra cut pieces.

Size	Fabric	Yardage	Cutting	Subcut
Baby	Pinks	¼ yard each of 6 fabrics	1 strip 7½˝ × fabric width from each fabric	5 squares 7½˝ × 7½˝ from each strip (30 total)
	Browns	¼ yard each of 3 fabrics	2 strips 3½˝ × fabric width from each fabric	6 strips 3½˝ × 6½˝ from each strip (30 total)
	Yellows	⅛ yard each of 2 fabrics	1 strip 3½˝ × fabric width from each fabric	16 strips 2½˝ × 3½˝ from each strip (30 total)
	White	⅝ yard	5 strips 3½˝ × fabric width	12 squares 3½˝ × 3½˝ from each strip (60 total)
	Backing	1⅝ yards		
	Binding	½ yard	5 strips 2½˝ × fabric width	
	Batting	41˝ × 52˝		
Crib	Pinks	¼ yard each of 10 fabrics	1 strip 7½˝ × fabric width from each fabric	5 squares 7½˝ × 7½˝ from each strip (48 total)
	Browns	¼ yard each of 4 fabrics	2 strips 3½˝ × fabric width from each fabric	6 strips 3½˝ × 6½˝ from each strip (48 total)
	Yellows	⅛ yard each of 3 fabrics	1 strip 3½˝ × fabric width from each fabric	16 strips 2½˝ × 3½˝ from each strip (48 total)
	White	⅞ yard	8 strips 3½˝ × fabric width	12 squares 3½˝ × 3½˝ from each strip (96 total)
	Backing	3⅛ yards		
	Binding	½ yard	6 strips 2½˝ × fabric width	
	Batting	53˝ × 62˝		

Size	Fabric	Yardage	Cutting	Subcut
Twin	Pinks	¼ yard each of 20 fabrics	1 strip 7½″ × fabric width from each fabric	5 squares 7½″ × 7½″ from each strip (99 total)
	Browns	¼ yard each of 9 fabrics	2 strips 3½″ × fabric width from each fabric	6 strips 3½″ × 6½″ from each strip (99 total)
	Yellows	⅛ yard each of 7 fabrics	1 strip 3½″ × fabric width from each fabric	16 strips 2½″ × 3½″ from each strip (99 total)
	White	1¾ yards	17 strips 3½″ × fabric width	12 squares 3½″ × 3½″ from each strip (198 total)
	Backing	5⅛ yards		
	Binding	⅝ yard	8 strips 2½″ × fabric width	
	Batting	71″ × 90″		

Block Assembly

Note that all sewing is done right sides together with a ¼″ seam allowance.

1. Place a pink 7½″ × 7½″ square right side up on the cutting mat. If you are using a directional print, place the square so the print's direction is horizontal. Make a vertical cut 3½″ from the right edge of the square (Figure 1).

2. Make a horizontal cut 1½″ from the top edge on the 3½″ strip. Make another cut 2½″ from the previous cut. You now have 1 strip 4″ × 7½″, 1 strip 1½″ × 3½″, 1 strip 2½″ × 3½″, and 1 square 3½″ × 3½″ (Figure 2).

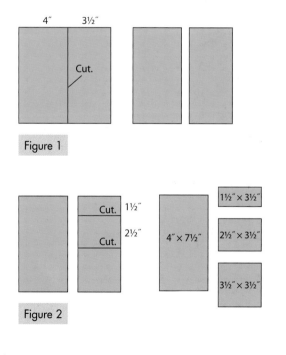

Figure 1

Figure 2

3. Replace the pink 2½˝ × 3½˝ strip with a yellow 2½˝ × 3½˝ strip. Sew the pieces of the 3½˝ strip back together and press the seams out. The strip measures 3½˝ × 6½˝ (Figure 3).

4. Line up the top edge of the 3½˝ strip with the top edge of the pink 4˝ × 7½˝ rectangle. Pin and sew the pieces together (Figure 4). Press toward the large rectangle and trim the bottom overhang so the block measures 6½˝ × 7˝ (Figure 5).

5. Draw a diagonal line in pencil from corner to corner on the wrong side of all the white 3½˝ squares (Figure 6). Place a white 3½˝ square right side down in the corner of a brown 3½˝ × 6½˝ strip (Figure 7). Pin and sew along the pencil line (Figure 8). Trim the corner, leaving a ¼˝ seam allowance (Figure 9), and press the corner seams out (Figure 10). Repeat with another white 3½˝ square in the opposite corner (Figure 11). The finished section measures 3½˝ × 6½˝ (Figure 12, page 59).

6. Align and pin the brown triangle section to the nonpieced 6½˝ side of the pink block. Sew the sections together and press toward the pink block (Figure 13, page 59). The unfinished block should measure 6½˝ × 10˝.

7. Make the following:

30 blocks for the baby size

48 blocks for the crib size

99 blocks for the twin size

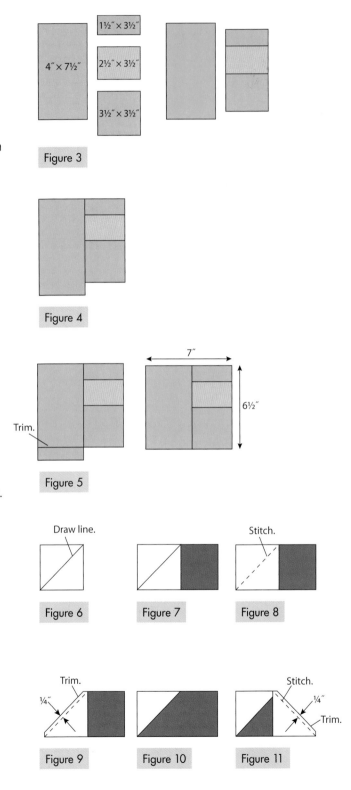

Figure 3

Figure 4

Figure 5

Figure 6   Figure 7   Figure 8

Figure 9   Figure 10   Figure 11

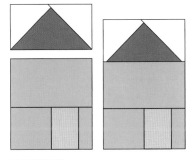

Figure 12

Figure 13

Finishing

Refer to Finishing the Quilt (pages 16–23) for information on making the backing, quilting, and binding the quilt.

Quilt Top Assembly

1. Lay out the blocks (Figure 14):

5 rows of 6 blocks for the baby size

6 rows of 8 blocks for the crib size

9 rows of 11 blocks for the twin size

2. Sew the blocks into rows and press the rows, alternating the pressing direction with each row. Sew the rows together and press to finish the quilt top.

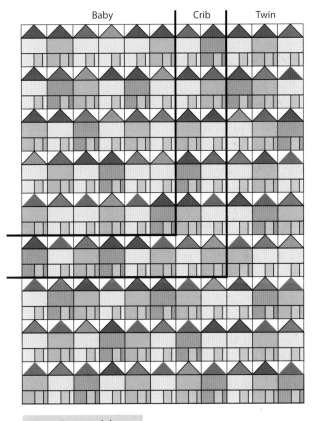

Figure 14—Quilt layout

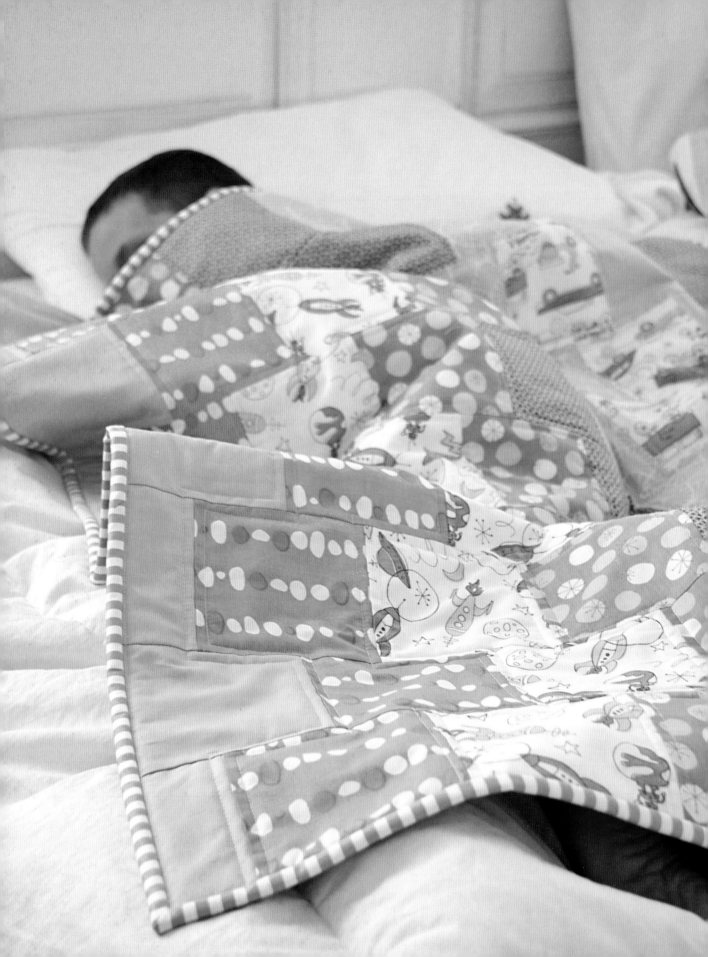

Stacks

Pieced and quilted by Allison Harris

Stacks *is a perfect beginner quilt. There aren't any complicated blocks to piece, there aren't any seams to match, and you'll get practice sewing the quilt top together. Plus it's fast to make! For the best results, choose a variety of small-scale prints, polka dots, and near-solids or solids to prevent this quilt from looking too busy.*

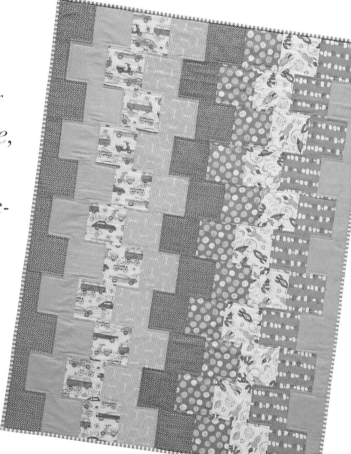

Focal fabrics shown are by Birch Fabrics.

FINISHED BABY QUILT: 38½″ × 50″

Yardage is based on 42˝-wide fabric unless noted. For this project, a fat quarter has a usable area of 18˝ × 21˝.

Fabric	Yardage	Cutting
Assorted prints and solids	9 fat quarters or ⅜ yard each of 9 fabrics	11 squares 5˝ × 5˝ from each fabric (99 total)* Optional: Cut and save 4 scrap 3˝ × 5˝ strips from each fabric to make the pieced backing (36 total).
Backing	Optional for pieced backing: 1½ yards print fabric, ½ yard coordinating solid, and scraps from the quilt front** OR 1⅝ yards***	Optional for pieced backing: Cut the *length* of the print fabric into a strip 14˝ × 47½˝ and a strip 25˝ × 47½˝. Cut the ½ yard solid fabric into 3 strips 5˝ × fabric width.
Binding	½ yard	5 strips 2½˝ × fabric width
Batting	43˝ × 54˝	

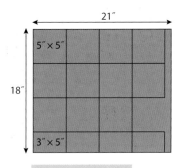

*Fat quarter cutting

**Optional for the pieced backing*

*** For one-piece backing, with 2˝ extra on each side, minimum 43˝ width of fabric*

Quilt Top Assembly

Note that all sewing is done right sides together with a ¼˝ seam allowance.

1. Place a 5˝ × 5˝ square from each of the 9 fabrics in the first row and arrange them as desired.

2. Cut the *last* 5˝ × 5˝ square in the row vertically in half, making 2 strips 2½˝ × 5˝.

Place one of the strips on the end of the first row and place the remaining strip at the end of Row 3.

3. Lay out Row 2 in the same order as you did Row 1, but this time cut the *first* square in half and place the cut half strip at the beginning of Row 4.

4. Continue laying out the squares in the same order, cutting the first and last squares in half as needed until the quilt has 11 rows of 9 blocks each.

5. Sew the blocks of each row together, pressing the seams in the same direction and alternating direction from row to row.

6. Sew the rows together and press the seams down toward the bottom of the quilt to finish the quilt top.

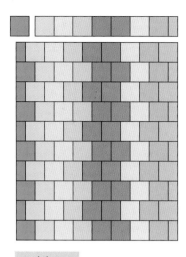

Quilt layout

Finishing

To make a one-piece or seamed simple backing, skip this step. To make the pieced backing, place the scrap 3″ × 5″ strips from each fat quarter into 3 rows of 11 strips each. As you did with the quilt top front, cut the last strips of Rows 1 and 3 vertically in half and discard a half from each strip. Then cut the first strip of Row 2 in half, leaving one of the halves in place. Sew the strips together along the 3″ sides to form rows. Press the seams to one side, alternating directions from row to row. From the 3 solid 5″ × fabric-width strips, piece together to make 2 strips that are 5″ × 47½″ long. Lay out the 14″ × 47½″ print strip, a 5″ × 47½″ solid strip, the 3 pieced strips (3″ × 47½″ each), the second solid 5″ × 47½″ strip, and the 25″ × 47½″ print strip. Sew the strips together to make the quilt back. Press well. The finished backing is slightly oversized. Trim as needed.

Refer to Making the Backing (page 17) for information on backings.

Refer to Finishing the Quilt (pages 16–23) for information on quilting and binding your quilt.

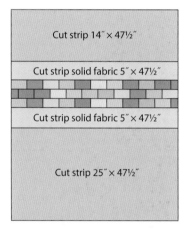

Cut strip 14″ × 47½″

Cut strip solid fabric 5″ × 47½″

Cut strip solid fabric 5″ × 47½″

Cut strip 25″ × 47½″

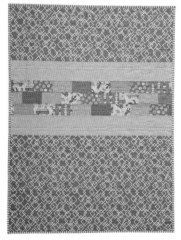

Optional pieced quilt back

The Color Block Quilt

Pieced and quilted by Allison Harris

My favorite type of quilt is bright, scrappy, and simple. So, there's no surprise that this is one of my very favorites.

FINISHED BABY QUILT: 38″ × 38″

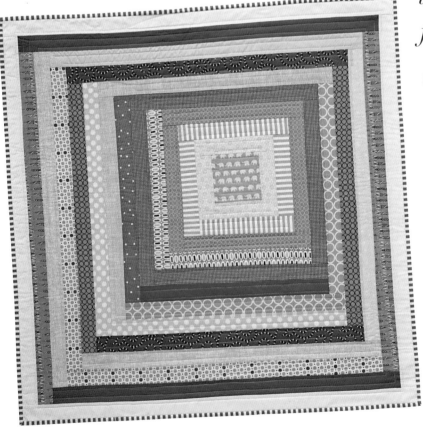

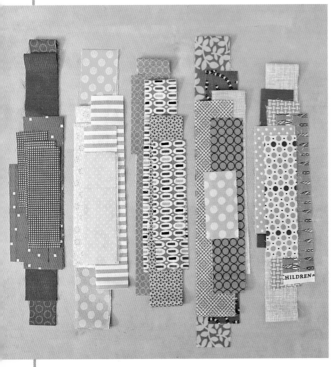

NOTE *If you want to use scraps, organize them into piles by color. Press and trim them into strips 2″ wide by however long the scrap is. Sew all the scraps from each color together into one long strip. Then press and cut, following the chart for each strip from that color. For a scrappier quilt, use shorter 2″ strips from more fabrics. In the cutting chart, I designated using two or three fabrics of colors in some color-ways. Mix and match the subcut strips as you like within that colorway to add interest to the quilt.*

Tip

If you don't want to cut all of the strips individually or if you aren't experienced at keeping a ¼″ seam allowance, you may want to measure and cut as you go instead of using the precise strip lengths.

Yardage is based on 42″-wide fabric. There is very little room for error when cutting the yardage and these strips. If the yardage or strips are cut crooked, you may need an extra 2″ of fabric to account for it.

Fabric	Yardage	Cutting	Subcut
Center fabric	5″ × 5″ square	5″ × 5″ square	
Light yellow	⅛ yard	1 strip 2″ × fabric width	1 strip 2″ × 5″ [1]* 2 strips 2″ × 6½″ [2, 3] 1 strip 2″ × 8″ [4]
Dark yellow	⅛ yard	1 strip 2″ × fabric width	1 strip 2″ × 8″ [5] 2 strips 2″ × 9½″ [6, 7] 1 strip 2″ × 11″ [8]

Fabric	Yardage	Cutting	Subcut
Orange	⅛ yard each of 2 fabrics	2 strips 2″ × fabric width from each fabric (4 total)	1 strip 2″ × 11″ [9] 2 strips 2″ × 12½″ [10, 11] 2 strips 2″ × 14″ [12, 13] 1 strip 2″ × 15½″ [14]
Red	⅛ yard each of 2 fabrics	2 strips 2″ × fabric width from each fabric (4 total)	1 strip 2″ × 15½″ [15] 2 strips 2″ × 17″ [16, 17] 2 strips 2″ × 18½″ [18, 19] 1 strip 2″ × 20″ [20]
Light green	⅛ yard each of 3 fabrics	2 strips 2″ × fabric width from each fabric (6 total)	1 strip 2″ × 20″ [21] 2 strips 2″ × 21½″ [22, 23] 2 strips 2″ × 23″ [24, 25] 1 strip 2″ × 24½″ [26]
Dark green	⅛ yard each of 2 fabrics	2 strips 2″ × fabric width from each fabric (4 total)	1 strip 2″ × 24½″ [27] 2 strips 2″ × 26″ [28, 29] 1 strip 2″ × 27½″ [30]
Light blue	⅛ yard each of 3 fabrics	2 strips 2″ × fabric width from each fabric (6 total)	1 strip 2″ × 27½″ [31] 2 strips 2″ × 29″ [32, 33] 2 strips 2″ × 30½″ [34, 35] 1 strip 2″ × 32″ [36]
Dark blue	⅛ yard each of 2 fabrics	2 strips 2″ × fabric width from each fabric (4 total)	1 strip 2″ × 32″ [37] 2 strips 2″ × 33½″ [38, 39] 1 strip 2″ × 35″ [40]
White	¼ yard	4 strips 2″ × fabric width	2 strips 2″ × 35″ 2 strips 2″ × 38″
Backing	1⅓ yards		
Binding	½ yard	5 strips 2½″ × fabric width	
Batting	42″ × 42″		

*The strip numbers appear in brackets [ ] and correspond with the strip numbers in the quilt layout diagram (page 68).

Quilt Top Assembly

Note that all sewing is done right sides together with a ¼˝ seam allowance.

1. Use the layout diagram to see the order in which to sew the strips onto the block. Find the number of the strip you are sewing on the diagram and then the coordinating number in the chart to see what length of strip to use.

2. Starting with Strip 1 (the 2˝ × 5˝ light yellow strip), pin, sew, and press the strip onto the center square. Continue with Strip 2 and so on through Strip 39, pressing the seams out as you go until all the strips are added.

3. Add Strip 40, press, and measure the block. It should measure 35˝ × 35˝ square at this point.

4. See Adding Borders (page 14) for information on adding the white side borders. Pin and sew a white 2˝ × 35˝ border strip to each side of the block. Press the seams toward the block.

5. Sew on the white 2˝ × 38˝ top and bottom borders. Press the seams toward the block.

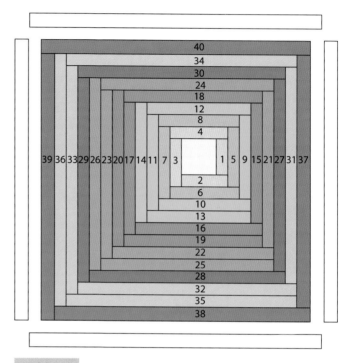

Quilt layout

Tip

If you are measuring as you go, you can measure, cut, and sew in the order on the layout diagram.

If you find that your strips are too long or too short when you go to sew them on, it is probably because your seam allowance is not exactly ¼˝. If the strips are too long, adjust your seam allowance to an exact ¼˝ or trim the excess as you go. If the strips are too short, sew an extra 2˝ scrap on to lengthen the strip. Or, if it is only a little shorter, pull and stretch the strip slightly. Gentle pressing will also help the block keep its shape as you sew.

Finishing

Refer to Finishing the Quilt (pages 16–23) for information on making the backing, quilting, and binding the quilt.

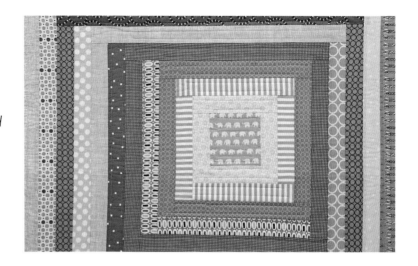

Tagged

Pieced by Allison Harris and quilted by Christina Lane

This quilt is perfect for showcasing special fabrics. Use fun novelty prints for the block centers to make a fun I-spy quilt!

FINISHED BLOCK: 8″ × 8″

FINISHED QUILT

BABY: 40″ × 49½″

CRIB: 49½″ × 59″

TWIN: 68½″ × 87½″

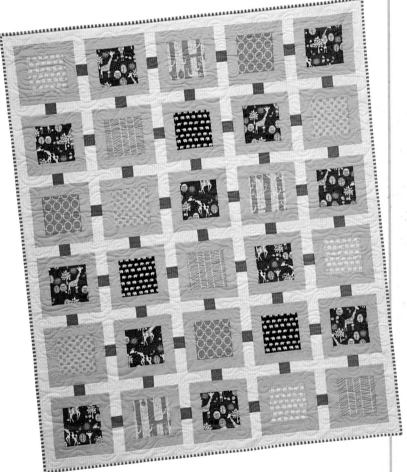

Quilt shown in a crib size

Yardage is based on 42″-wide fabric. In some cases, you might have a few extra cut pieces.

Size	Fabric	Yardage	Cutting	Subcut
Baby	Prints	20 assorted 5½″ × 5½″ squares		
	White	⅞ yard	4 strips 3¾″ × fabric width	
			6 strips 2″ × fabric width	1 strip into 12 squares 2″ × 2″
	Blue	1 yard	10 strips 2″ × fabric width	4 strips 2″ × 8½″ from each strip (40 total)
			6 strips 2″ × fabric width	7 strips 2″ × 5½″ from each strip (40 total)
	Red	⅛ yard	2 strips 2″ × fabric width	
	Backing	2⅝ yards		
	Binding	½ yard	5 strips 2½″ × fabric width	
	Batting	44″ × 54″		
Crib	Prints	30 assorted 5½″ × 5½″ squares		
	White	1⅛ yards	6 strips 3¾″ × fabric width	
			7 strips 2″ × fabric width	1 strip into 20 squares 2″ × 2″
	Blue	1½ yards	15 strips 2″ × fabric width	4 strips 2″ × 8½″ from each strip (60 total)
			9 strips 2″ × fabric width	7 strips 2″ × 5½″ from each strip (60 total)
	Red	¼ yard	3 strips 2″ × fabric width	
	Backing	3⅛ yards		
	Binding	½ yard	6 strips 2½″ × fabric width	
	Batting	54″ × 63″		

Size	Fabric	Yardage	Cutting	Subcut
Twin	Prints	63 assorted 5½˝ × 5½˝ squares; OR 7 fat quarters; OR 7 regular cuts ⅜ yard each	If using fat quarters, cut 9 squares 5½˝ × 5½˝* from each fabric. If using regular cuts, cut 9 squares 5½˝ × 5½˝ from each fabric.	
	White	2 yards	12 strips 3¾˝ × fabric width	
			11 strips 2˝ × fabric width	3 strips into 48 squares 2˝ × 2˝
	Blue	2⅞ yards	32 strips 2˝ × fabric width	4 strips 2˝ × 8½˝ from each strip (126 total)
			18 strips 2˝ × fabric width	7 strips 2˝ × 5½˝ from each strip (126 total)
	Red	½ yard	6 strips 2˝ × fabric width	
	Backing	5¼ yards		
	Binding	¾ yard	9 strips 2½˝ × fabric width	
	Batting	73˝ × 92˝		

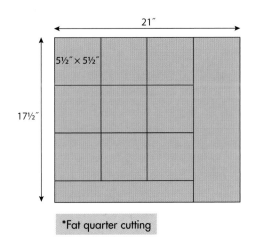

*Fat quarter cutting

Block Assembly

Note that all sewing is done right sides together with a ¼˝ seam allowance.

1. Pin and sew a blue 2˝ × 5½˝ strip to each side of the 5½˝ × 5½˝ squares. Press the seams out (Figure 1).

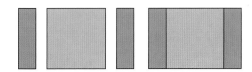

Figure 1

2. Pin and sew a blue 2″ × 8½″ strip to the top and bottom of each block (Figure 2). Press the seams out.

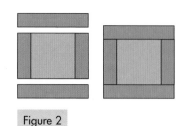

Figure 2

3. Repeat Steps 1 and 2 to make 20 blocks 8½″ × 8½″ for the baby size, 30 blocks for the crib size, or 63 blocks for the twin size.

4. Sew a white 3¾″ × fabric-width strip to each side of a red 2″ strip (Figure 3). Press the seams toward the center. The pieced strip set measures 8½″ × fabric width. Repeat until you've made 2 sets for the baby size, 3 sets for the crib size, or 6 sets for the twin size.

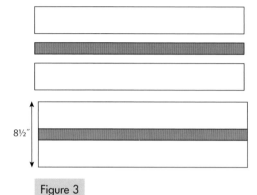

8½″

Figure 3

5. Cut 2″ × 8½″ sashing strips from each strip set from Step 4 (Figure 4). Cut:

31 strips for the baby size

49 strips for the crib size

110 strips for the twin size

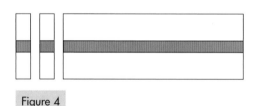

Figure 4

Quilt Top Assembly

1. Lay out the blocks (Figure 5):

5 rows of 4 blocks for the baby size

6 rows of 5 blocks for the crib size

9 rows of 7 blocks for the twin size

2. Place a 2″ × 8½″ vertical sashing strip between each block.

3. Sew the blocks and sashing strips together to make each row. Press seams toward the blocks.

4. Make a row for the horizontal sashing strips by laying out:

4 white-and-red 2″ × 8½″ sashing strips for the baby size

5 white-and-red 2″ × 8½″ sashing strips for the crib size

7 white-and-red 2″ × 8½″ sashing strips for the twin size.

Place a 2″ × 2″ white square between each sashing strip.

5. Sew the strips and squares together to make each horizontal sashing strip. Press the seams toward the sashing strips.

6. Repeat Steps 4 and 5 to make the following:

4 horizontal strips for the baby size

5 horizontal strips for the crib size

8 horizontal strips for the twin size

7. Place a horizontal sashing strip between each row from Step 3. Pin and sew the rows and horizontal sashing strips together to make the quilt center. Press the seams toward the blocks.

8. Sew the white 2″ × fabric-width strips together end to end to create a long strip to be used for the borders.

9. See Adding Borders (page 14) to measure the sides of the quilt top. Mark that length with a pin and then cut along the 2″ border strip. The approximate lengths are as follows:

46½″ for the baby size

56″ for the crib size

84½″ for the twin size

Pin and sew the border strip to one side of the quilt top. Mark and trim to add the second side border.

10. Similarly, measure the quilt along the top and bottom and repeat the steps to mark and attach the top and bottom border. The approximate top and bottom borders measure as follows:

40″ for the baby size

49½″ for the crib size

68½ for the twin size

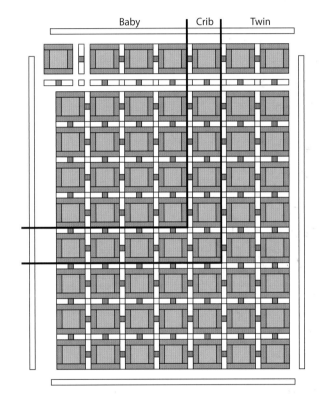

Figure 5—Quilt layout

Note: All sizes have an outer border surrounding the quilt center.

Finishing

Refer to Finishing the Quilt (pages 16–23) for information on making the backing, quilting, and binding the quilt.

Tagged

Sparkle

Pieced by Allison Harris and quilted by Christina Lane

Classic hourglass blocks give this pattern its fun shape. The blocks are simple to make with this easy method.

FINISHED BLOCK: 4″ × 4″

FINISHED BABY QUILT: 43½″ × 49½″

The print fabric is Daisy Cottage by Bee in My Bonnet for Riley Blake Designs.

Yardage is based on 42″-wide fabric. In some cases, you might have a few extra cut pieces so you can adjust colors as you like.

Fabric	Yardage	Cutting	Subcut
Prints	¼ yard each of 7 fabrics	1 strip 5½″ × fabric width from each fabric*	3** squares 5½″ × 5½″; trim remainder of strip to 4½″ wide and cut 5 squares 4½″ × 4½″ from each fabric
Solid for background and inner border	1 yard	3 strips 5½″ × fabric width	6 squares 5½″ × 5½″ from each strip (18 total)
		7 strips 1½″ × fabric width	9 strips 1½″ × 4½″ from each strip (60 total)
		4 strips 1½″ × fabric width (inner border)	
Outer border	⅔ yard	5 strips 4″ × fabric width	
Backing	2⅞ yards		
Binding	Scraps from the print fabrics or ½ yard	Scrap binding: 7 strips 2½″ × fabric width from the print scraps; cut the strips in half twice to make 28 strips 2½″ × 10½″. *Optional:* For a nonscrap binding, cut 5 strips 2½″ × fabric width.	
Batting	48″ × 54″		

*** I cut 3 squares of each fabric to have more color choices.*

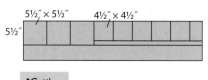

*Cutting

Handwritten margin notes: total. 5½ × 2 4½ × 5

Block Assembly

Note that all sewing is done right sides together with a ¼˝ seam allowance.

1. On the wrong side of 18 of the 5½˝ × 5½˝ print squares, draw a diagonal line from corner to corner in pencil. Place a background solid square and a print square right sides together and pin. Sew ¼˝ on each side of the pencil line (Figure 1). Note that the starting squares are slightly oversized; you will trim the hourglass blocks to the proper size in Step 6. This allows more "wiggle room" when constructing the blocks.

2. Cut on the pencil line. *Do not move the squares yet!* Without moving the squares, make another cut from the opposite corner to corner, making 4 triangles (Figure 1).

Figure 1

3. Open and press the seams toward the print fabric. You should have 2 triangles with the print on the left side and 2 triangles with the print on the right side (Figure 2).

4. Repeat Steps 1–3 with the remaining 5½˝ × 5½˝ print and background squares.

5. Choose 2 different coordinating triangles to make an hourglass block; pin and sew the halves together. Press the seams open to reduce bulk. Make 35 blocks.

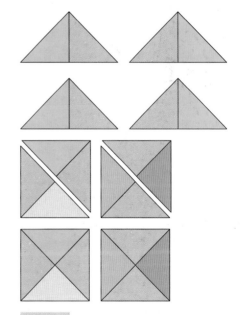

Figure 2

6. Square up each unfinished hourglass block to 4½˝ × 4½˝ (Figure 2).

Quilt Top Assembly

1. Lay out the blocks in 10 rows of 7 blocks, alternating between a print 4½˝ × 4½˝ square and an hourglass block (Figure 3).

2. Place a solid 1½˝ × 4½˝ background strip between each of the blocks in each row. Sew the blocks and strips together to make the rows. Alternate the direction of pressing the seams toward either the blocks or the background strips from row to row (for example, press Row 1 seams toward the blocks, Row 2 seams toward the solid strips, Row 3 toward the blocks, and so on).

3. Match the seams, pin, and sew the rows together to make the quilt top center. I recommend pressing the seams open to reduce bulk, but you can also press them in either direction.

4. See Adding Borders (page 14) to measure the quilt top from top to bottom along the sides and in the center. Cut 2 inner border strips to that length (approximately 40½˝); then pin and sew the strips to each side of the quilt center. Press the seams out.

5. Repeat Step 4 to add the top and bottom inner border, this time measuring along the top, bottom, and center of the quilt (approximately 36½˝).

6. Sew the outer border strips together end to end to make a long strip. Press the seams. Measure the quilt top and add borders as you did with the inner border, but cut the borders from the long strip. Side borders are approximately 42½˝, and the top and bottom borders are approximately 43½˝. Press the seams out to finish the quilt top.

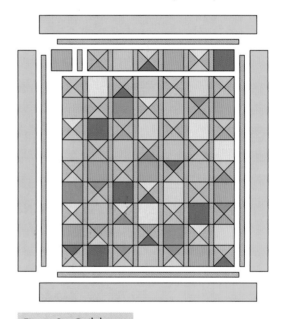

Figure 3—Quilt layout

Finishing

Refer to Finishing the Quilt (pages 16–23) for information on making the backing, quilting, and binding the quilt. For the scrappy binding, I sewed my scrappy strips together on the diagonal. You need about 200˝ of binding to complete the quilt.

Sparkle

Scrappy Reader Pillow

Made by Allison Harris

This fun little pillow makes a perfect place to store a favorite book or prop a head while you read. It's a great way to use up a handful of scraps, and it makes a great gift with a book tucked inside.

FINISHED PILLOW: 14˝ x 14˝

Fabric	Yardage	Cutting
Pocket front	28 squares 2½″ × 2½″ of assorted fabrics	
Pillow front fabric	1 fat quarter or ½ yard	1 square 14½″ × 14½″
Pillow backing and pocket backing	½ yard	2 rectangles 10″ × 14½″ 1 rectangle 8½″ × 14½″
Batting	8½″ × 14½″	
Pillow form	14″ × 14″	

Making the Pocket

Note that all sewing is done right sides together with a ¼″ seam allowance.

1. Lay out the 2½″ print squares into 4 rows of 7 squares. Sew the squares into rows, alternating the pressing direction for each row. Pin and sew the rows together (Figure 1). Press the seams down in one direction. The pocket front should measure 8½″ × 14½″.

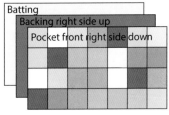

Figure 1

2. Lay the batting down flat and place the 8½″ × 14½″ backing rectangle and the pocket front *right sides together* onto the batting (Figure 2). Pin and sew along the top edge through all 3 layers, using a ¼″ seam allowance.

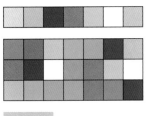

Figure 2

3. Open and separate the pocket front and the backing, press the edge of the pocket front away from the center, and flip the pocket front over to the exposed side of the batting right side out. Press the edge and topstitch along the top, ¼″ from the edge (Figure 3).

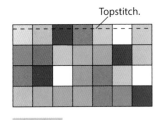

Figure 3

4. Quilt the pocket front as desired through all 3 layers (Figure 4).

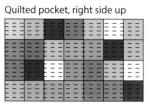

Quilted pocket, right side up

Figure 4

Making the Pillow

1. On each 10″ × 14½″ backing rectangle, fold one of the 14½″ edges in ¼″ toward the wrong side of the fabric and press; then fold again ½″ and press to make a hem. Topstitch to catch the first folded edge and press again to finish the hemmed edges (Figure 5).

Backing wrong side

Figure 5

2. Lay the pillow front square right side up and place the quilted pocket right side up on top of the pillow front, matching the bottom and side edges. Place a backing rectangle right side down so it covers half of the pillow, with the hemmed edge toward the center. Place the other backing rectangle on the other side of the pillow, right side down, with the hemmed edge toward the center (Figure 6). Match all raw edges and pin through all 3 layers.

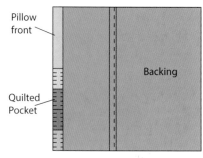

Pillow front

Quilted Pocket

Backing

Figure 6

3. Sew around the pillow using a ¼″ seam allowance (Figure 7). For extra durability, zigzag stitch (or serge) around the outside edges to prevent fraying. Trim the corners at an angle and turn the pillow right side out. Press the edges.

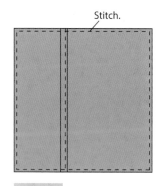

Stitch.

Figure 7

4. Place the 14″ × 14″ pillow form into the pillow cover and remove some stuffing from the pillow form if needed. Place a book in the pocket and enjoy!

Urban

Pieced and quilted by Allison Harris

This quilt makes a perfect last-minute baby gift because it goes together quickly and doesn't require a lot of fabric cuts. Choose three prints to make the blocks, or use scraps to make it even better. Switch it up by using solids instead of prints for the blocks and a large print for the background.

FINISHED BLOCK: 12″ × 12″

FINISHED BABY QUILT: 36½″ × 42″

Yardage is based on 42"-wide fabric.

Fabric	Yardage	Cutting*	Subcut
Prints	¼ yard each of 3 fabrics	1 strip 2½" × fabric width from each fabric	3 squares 2½" × 2½", 2 strips 2½" × 6½", and 2 strips 2½" × 8½" from each strip
		1 strip 2½" × fabric width from each fabric	2 strips 2½" × 12½" from each strip
		1 strip 1½" × fabric width from each fabric	2 strips 1½" × 6½" and 2 strips 1½" × 8½" from each strip
Solid	⅞ yard	1 strip 18½" × 42" 1 strip 6½" × 42"	
		1 strip 1¾" × fabric width	2 strips 1¾" × 12½"
		1 strip 2" × fabric width	2 strips 2" × 12½"
Backing	1½ yards		
Binding	½ yard or use scraps	5 strips 2½" × fabric width, or sew scraps together to make a binding strip at least 2½" × 170"	
Batting	41" × 46"		

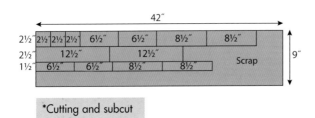

*Cutting and subcut

Block Assembly

Note that all sewing is done right sides together with a ¼″ seam allowance.

1. Choose a 2½″ × 2½″ square for the center of a block. From a second fabric, choose 2 squares 2½″ × 2½″ and 2 strips 2½″ × 6½″. Sew the 2½″ × 2½″ squares of the second fabric onto each side of the center square and press the seams out (Figure 1). Sew the 2½″ × 6½″ strips to the top and bottom of the block and press the seams out (Figure 2).

2. From a third fabric, sew the 1½″ × 6½″ strips to each side of the block and press the seams out (Figure 3). Sew the 1½″ × 8½″ strips to the top and bottom of the block and press the seams out (Figure 4).

3. From the same fabric used for your center square, sew the 2½″ × 8½″ strips to each side of the block and press the seams out (Figure 5).

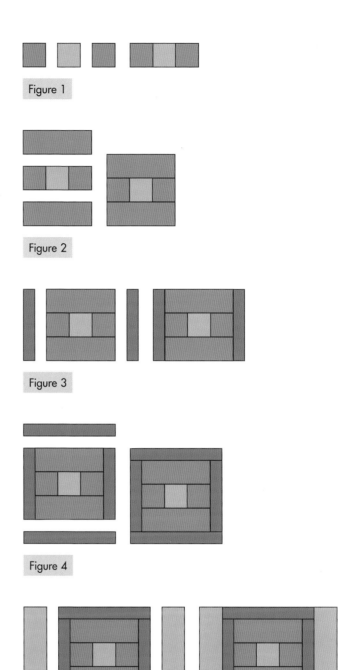

Figure 1

Figure 2

Figure 3

Figure 4

Figure 5

4. Sew the 2½″ × 12½″ strips to the top and bottom of the block and press the seams out (Figure 6). The block measures 12½″ × 12½″.

5. Repeat Steps 1–4 to make 2 more blocks, until all the fabrics have been used as the center and surrounding bands of the blocks (Figure 7).

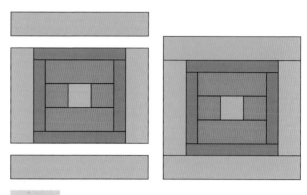

Figure 6

Quilt Top Assembly

1. Lay out the 3 blocks vertically in a column (Figure 8). Sew a 2″ × 12½″ background strip to the top of the first block and the bottom of the last block in the column. Press the seams toward the strips. Sew the 1¾″ × 12½″ background strips between the blocks to make the column; press.

2. Pin and sew the 18½″ × 42″ strip to the left side of the blocks column. Sew the 6½″ × 42″ strip to the right side of the blocks column. Press the seams toward the solid strips.

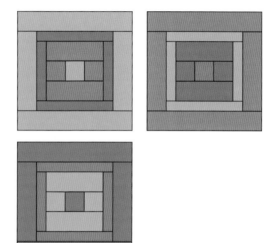

Figure 7

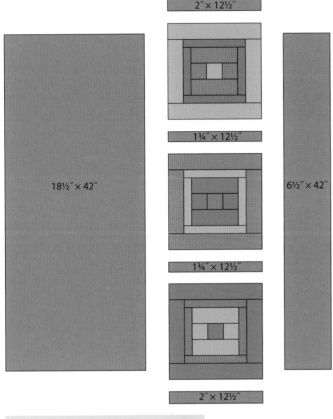

Figure 8—Quilt layout. Cut sizes shown.

Finishing

*Refer to Finishing the Quilt (pages 16–23)
for information on making the backing,
quilting, and binding the quilt.*

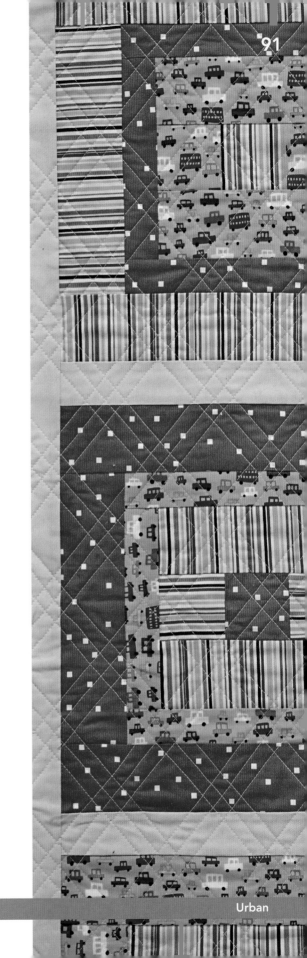

Back to School

Pieced and quilted by Allison Harris

Everybody loves a fresh box of colored pencils to play with, and now you can snuggle up with them! This quilt is perfect for a budding artist, a teacher's wallhanging, or a cozy reading nook. It is easy to make larger or smaller by adding more "pencils" until it's as big as you want!

FINISHED BLOCK: 3½" × 10" • FINISHED BABY QUILT: 38½" × 43½"

Yardage is based on 42″-wide fabric.

Fabric	Yardage	Cutting	Subcut
Solids	¼ yard each of 6 fabrics	1 strip 4″ × fabric width of each fabric	4 strips 4″ × 8″ and 4 strips 2″ × 4″ from each strip (24 total of each size)
Tan	¼ yard	3 strips 1½″ × fabric width	8 strips 1½″ × 4″ from each strip (24 total)
White	¾ yard	6 strips 2″ × fabric width for the sashings and inner border	
		4 strips 3″ × fabric width	12 squares 3″ × 3″ from each strip (48 total)
Border	⅝ yard	4 strips 4″ × fabric width	
Backing	1½ yards		
Binding	½ yard	5 strips 2½″ × fabric width	
Batting	43″ × 48″		

Block Assembly

Note that all sewing is done right sides together with a ¼˝ seam allowance.

1. Sew each of the solid 2˝ × 4˝ strips to a tan 1½˝ × 4˝ strip and press (Figure 1).

2. Draw a diagonal line in pencil from corner to corner on the wrong side of the 48 white 3˝ × 3˝ squares (Figure 2).

3. Lay a square right side down in the corner of the sewn strip. Pin and sew along the pencil line and trim the corner, leaving a ¼˝ seam allowance (Figure 2). Press the seam open.

4. Repeat Step 3 with the opposite corner and another 3˝ × 3˝ square (Figure 3).

5. Repeat Steps 1–4 until you have made 24 pencil points measuring 3˝ × 4˝.

6. Sew each point to a 4˝ × 8˝ rectangle of the same color. Press the seams toward the large rectangle (Figure 4).

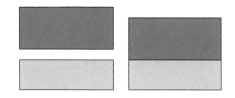

Figure 1

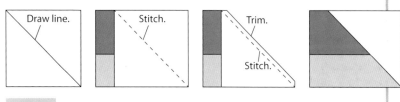

Figure 2

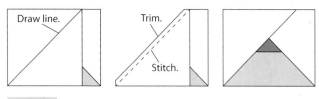

Figure 3

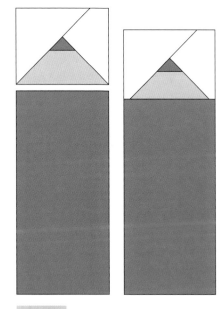

Figure 4

Quilt Top Assembly

1. Arrange the blocks in 3 rows of 8 blocks (Figure 5). Match and pin the seams. Sew the blocks into rows and press the seams open to reduce bulk.

2. Measure the 3 rows and cut 2 of the white 2″ × fabric-width strips to that length (approximately 28½″). If the rows differ slightly in length, use the average length.

3. Sew a white strip between each row. Press the seams toward the blocks.

4. Refer to Adding Borders (page 14) to measure both sides and the center of the quilt top. Mark that length (approximately 33½″) with a pin along 2 of the white 2″ × fabric-width strips. Pin and sew a white strip to each side of the quilt and trim any excess. Press the seams toward the border.

5. Measure the quilt along the top, bottom, and center and repeat the steps to mark and attach the top and bottom inner border. The top and bottom borders measure approximately 31½″.

6. Repeat Steps 4 and 5 to measure, mark, and sew the outer border strips to the quilt top. Each side border measures approximately 36½″, and the top and bottom borders measure approximately 38½″. Press the seams toward the edges of the quilt top.

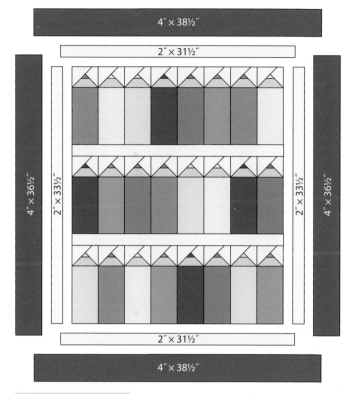

Figure 5—Quilt layout

Within the layout diagram:

- 4″ × 38½″ (top)
- 2″ × 31½″ (top inner)
- 4″ × 36½″ (left outer)
- 2″ × 33½″ (left inner)
- 2″ × 33½″ (right inner)
- 4″ × 36½″ (right outer)
- 2″ × 31½″ (bottom inner)
- 4″ × 38½″ (bottom)

Finishing

Refer to Finishing the Quilt (pages 16–23) for information on making the backing, quilting, and binding the quilt.

Tick Tock

Pieced by Allison Harris and quilted by Dianne Rencher

Strip piecing makes this a fast, simple, beginner-friendly project. This pattern comes in three sizes and works well for any age.

FINISHED BLOCK: 6½″ × 6½″

FINISHED QUILT

BABY: 33″ × 39½″

CRIB: 46″ × 52½″

TWIN: 65½″ × 85″

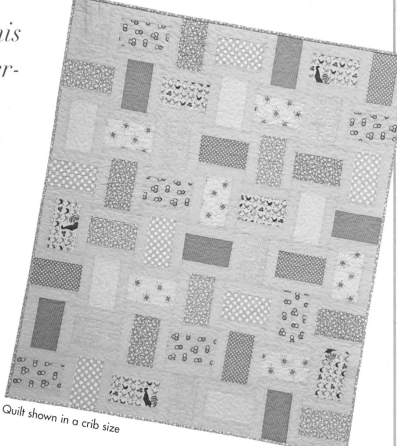

Quilt shown in a crib size

Yardage is based on 42″-wide fabric. There is very little room for error when cutting the print yardage and their strips. If the yardage is cut crooked, you may need extra fabric so that you can cut 4″ strips.

Size	Fabric	Yardage	Cutting
Baby	Prints	⅛ yard each of 5 fabrics	1 strip 4″ × fabric width from each fabric (5 total)
	Background	⅝ yard	10 strips 2″ × fabric width
	Backing	1⅜ yards	
	Binding	⅜ yard	4 strips 2½″ × fabric width
	Batting	37″ × 44″	
Crib	Prints	⅛ yard each of 10 fabrics	1 strip 4″ × fabric width from each fabric (10 total)
	Background	1¼ yards	20 strips 2″ × fabric width
	Backing	3 yards	
	Binding	½ yard	6 strips 2½″ × fabric width
	Batting	50″ × 57″	
Twin	Prints	⅛ yard each of 22 fabrics, *OR* ¼ yard each of 11 fabrics	Cut each ⅛ yard into a strip 4″ × fabric width, or cut each ¼ yard into 2 strips 4″ × fabric width (22 total).
	Background	2⅝ yards	44 strips 2″ × fabric width
	Backing	5⅛ yards	
	Binding	⅝ yard	8 strips 2½″ × fabric width
	Batting	70″ × 89″	

Block Assembly

Note that all sewing is done right sides together with a ¼″ seam allowance.

Tip

Speed things up by chain piecing the strips together one after another without stopping to clip the threads. Refer to Chain Piecing (page 13).

1. Sew a 2″-wide solid background strip onto both sides of each 4″-wide print strip (Figure 1). Repeat until you've made 5 sets for the baby size, 10 sets for the crib size, or 22 sets for the twin size.

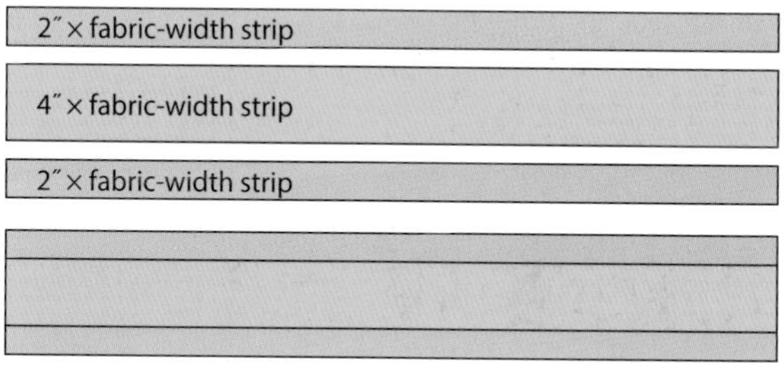

2. Press the seams toward the print strip if you are using a light background fabric or away from it if your background fabric is dark.

3. Cut each strip set into 6 squares 7″ × 7″ (Figure 2) to make:

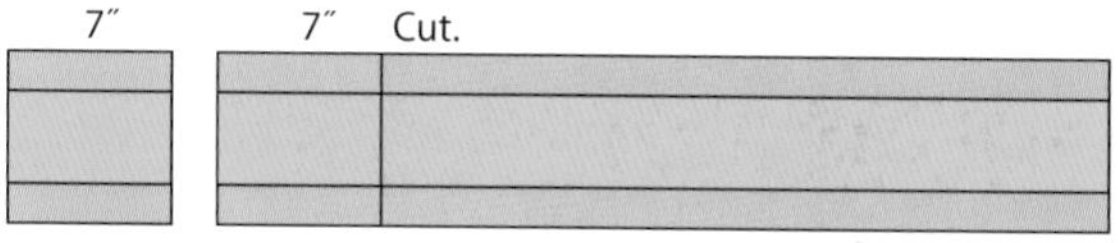

30 blocks for the baby size

56 blocks for the crib size

130 blocks for the twin size

(You may have a few extra blocks if you cut all the strip sets into 6 squares, depending on the size quilt you are making.)

2″ × fabric-width strip

4″ × fabric-width strip

2″ × fabric-width strip

Figure 1

7″   7″   Cut.

Figure 2

Quilt Top Assembly

1. Lay out the blocks as follows (Figure 3):

6 rows of 5 blocks for the baby size

8 rows of 7 blocks for the crib size

13 rows of 10 blocks for the twin size

2. Rotate every other block 90°. Sew the blocks into rows and press, alternating the pressing direction for each row.

3. Sew the rows together and press well to finish the quilt top.

Figure 3—Quilt layout

Finishing

Refer to Finishing the Quilt (pages 16–23) for information on making the backing, quilting, and binding the quilt.

Quillow

Pieced and quilted by Allison Harris

A quilt that folds into a pillow = a quillow! Quillows are great to take on trips, stow in the car for on-the-go nap-times, or enjoy on the couch. When these quil-lows are unfolded, little feet can fit in the pocket at the end for extra warmth. Use a thin batting, or skip the batting altogether and use a soft chenille or fleece for the backing.

FINISHED CRIB QUILT: 41″ × 57″ • FINISHED PILLOW SIZE: 15½″ × 15½″

Yardage is based on 42″-wide fabric. Some quantities are tight, and there is not much extra for crooked cuts.

Fabric	Yardage	Cutting
Front	1¾ yards	42″ × 58″
Pocket front (visible when the quilt is folded)	1 fat quarter or ½ yard	17″ × 17″
Pocket back (visible on the back of the quilt when it's unfolded)	1 fat quarter or ½ yard	17″ × 17″
Backing	1¾ yards	42″ × 58″
Batting	42″ × 58″ and 17″ × 17″	
Fabric or webbing for the handle	10″ cotton webbing or make a handle from a 5″ × 10″ scrap of fabric	

Quilt Assembly

Use a ½″ seam allowance unless noted.

1. Lay the 42″ × 58″ batting on the floor and place the backing and quilt front *right sides together* on top of the batting (Figure 1). Make sure the edges are even; then pin the edges well.

2. Using a ½″ seam allowance and a walking foot, sew around the entire quilt, leaving an 8″ opening in one side for turning (Figure 2). Trim the excess fabric from the corners at an angle, turn the quilt right side out gently, and pin the hole shut. Press the edges well and topstitch around the entire quilt ¼″ from the edges, making sure to close the hole with the topstitching.

3. With a walking foot, loosely quilt the layers every 3″–6″—just enough to keep the layers from shifting (refer to Machine Quilting on page 19). Too much quilting will make the quilt stiff and harder to fold into the pocket.

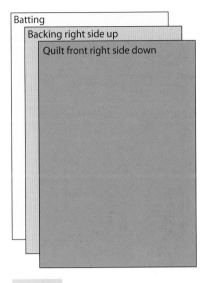

Batting
Backing right side up
Quilt front right side down

Figure 1

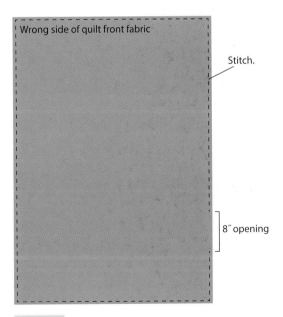

Wrong side of quilt front fabric

Stitch.

8″ opening

Figure 2

Pocket Assembly

1. Use the cotton webbing for the handle. Or if you are making the handle, cut a strip 5″ × 10″ from a scrap. Press both of the 10″ edges of the strip into the center and press; then fold the strip in half to make 1 strip 1¼″ × 10″. Topstitch to secure the edges together.

Batting

Pocket back right side up

Figure 3

2. Lay the 17″ × 17″ pocket batting down and place the pocket back *right side up* on the batting (Figure 3).

Figure 4

3. Find the center of the top edge of the pocket back, and arrange the handle so the raw edges match up with the edges of the pocket back and the top of the handle is toward the center. Pin the handle in place (down), keeping the pins away from where you'll be sewing (Figure 4).

Pocket front right side down

Figure 5

4. Place the pocket front square *right side down* on top of the backing material and handle (Figure 5). Match the edges and pin well.

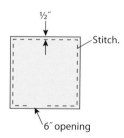

½″

Stitch.

6″ opening

Figure 6

5. Using a ½″ seam allowance and a walking foot, sew around the edges, leaving a 6″ opening in the bottom—that is, the side opposite the handle (Figure 6). Trim the corners, gently turn right side out, press the edges well, and pin the hole closed.

6. Topstitch along the edge of the pocket bottom (with the opening), making sure to close the opening with the stitches (Figure 7). Optionally, stitch a second row of topstitching all around, ¼″ in from the first topstitching.

Top stitch.

Figure 7

7. Quilt the pocket as desired.

Attaching the Pocket

1. Pin the handle down toward the center of the pocket front fabric. Keep the handle pinned down until the pocket is sewn on.

2. Lay the quilt on the floor with the *quilt back side up.* Place the pocket along the bottom edge, exactly centered and with the pocket front fabric *right side down.* Arrange the pocket so that the top portion with the handle is just above the quilt's *bottom edge.*

3. Pin the pocket to the quilt, leaving the edge of the pocket that faces the quilt center open. Sew around the remaining 3 sides of the pillow, ¼˝ from the edge, using a walking foot (Figure 8). Backstitch well at either side of the pillow opening.

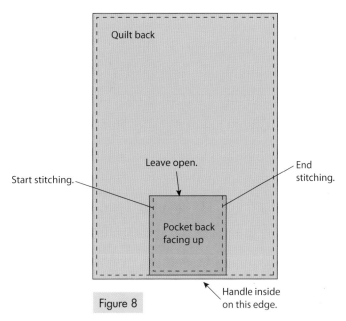

Quilt back

Start stitching.

Leave open.

End stitching.

Pocket back facing up

Handle inside on this edge.

Figure 8

Folding the Quillow

1. Place the quillow on the floor *right side up*. Fold the quilt length about in thirds, using the edges of the pocket as a guide (Figure 9).

2. Fold the quillow about into fourths. On the last fold (Figure 10), flip the quilt over, reach into the pocket, and turn the pillow portion inside out over the folded quilt (Figure 11). It may take some working to get the quilt to fill out the pillow and the corners, but after a few times, it will become easier.

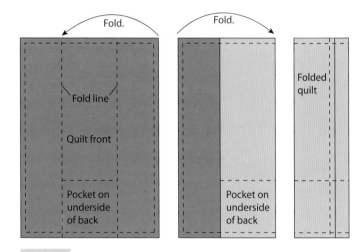

Fold.

Fold.

Fold line

Quilt front

Pocket on underside of back

Pocket on underside of back

Folded quilt

Figure 9

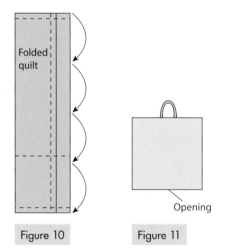

Folded quilt

Opening

Figure 10

Figure 11

Quillow

Rock-a-Baby

Pieced and quilted by Allison Harris

Stack-and-cut block assembly makes this quilt fun to put together and will add a modern splash of color to a baby's room. If you've never pieced an angled seam, these blocks are a good way to learn and are fast to make.

FINISHED BLOCK: 4½" × 4½"

FINISHED BABY QUILT: 41" × 46½"

Yardage is based on 42″-wide fabric. Fat quarters have a usable area of 18″ × 21″.

Fabric	Yardage	Cutting	Subcut
Prints and solids	7 fat quarters or ⅜ yard of 7 fabrics	8 squares 6″ × 6″ from each fabric*	
White	1 yard	6 strips 1½″ × fabric width	8 strips 1½″ × 5″ (48 total)
		7 strips 1½″ × fabric width for horizontal sashing	
		5 strips 2″ × fabric width for borders	
Backing	1½ yards** 2⅔ yards***		
Binding	½ yard	5 strips 2½″ × fabric width	
Batting	45″ × 51″		

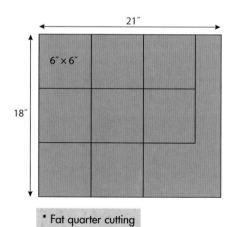

21″

6″ × 6″

18″

* Fat quarter cutting

** If the fabric is at least 45″ wide.

*** If the fabric is less than 45″ wide

Block Assembly

Note that all sewing is done right sides together with a ¼″ seam allowance.

1. Place a 6″ × 6″ square right side up on the cutting mat. Measure 2½″ along the top and 1½″ along the bottom, both from the right side of the square (Figure 1). Mark or eyeball the measurements, align your cutting ruler along both points, and make an angled cut.

2. Continue making the same cut through all of the 6″ × 6″ squares, keeping the large wedges together and the small wedges together.

Tip

You can stack three or more squares and cut them at once to speed things up.

3. Pin and sew the pieces back together, mixing the fabrics (Figure 2). Press the seams toward the small wedges. When placed right sides together before sewing, the top corner of the wedge will slightly overhang the large piece. However, the top edges meet at the seamline (Figure 3), and when sewn and pressed, they will align. *Don't worry too much about getting the edges perfectly aligned because you'll be trimming the top and bottom edges later.* Continue until all of the squares are sewn back together and have 2 fabrics (Figure 4).

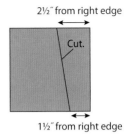

2½″ from right edge

Cut.

1½″ from right edge

Figure 1

Figure 2

Stitch.

Figure 3

Figure 4

4. Place a pieced square right side up on the cutting mat and measure 2½″ along the top and 1½″ along the bottom, both from the left edge (Figure 5). Mark or eyeball the points, align the ruler, and make a cut. Continue cutting through all of the blocks in the same manner.

5. As with Step 3, mix fabrics and sew a wedge onto all of the blocks (Figure 5). Press the seams toward the small wedge. Continue until you have 56 blocks.

6. The blocks measure 5″ × 6″ (Figure 6). Trim ½″ from the top and bottom of each block (Figure 7) to make each unfinished block 5″ × 5″ (Figure 8).

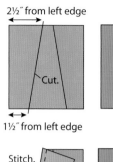
2½″ from left edge

Cut.

1½″ from left edge

Stitch.

Figure 5

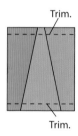

Figure 6

Trim.

Trim.

Figure 7

Figure 8

Quilt Top Assembly

1. Lay out the blocks into 8 rows of 7 blocks (Figure 9). Rotate the blocks as desired.

2. Place a white 1½″ × 5″ strip between each of the blocks in each row. Pin and sew the blocks and strips together to make the rows. Press the seams toward the blocks.

3. Measure each row, take the average (approximately 38″), and cut 7 of the white 1½″ × fabric-width strips to that length. Place a white strip between each row; then pin and sew the rows and strips together. Press the seams toward the rows.

4. Join the 5 strips 2″ × fabric width together end to end. Press the seams open. Refer to Adding Borders (page 14) to measure the quilt top along the sides and in the center. Cut 2 strips to that length (approximately 43½″); pin and sew the strips to either side of the quilt center. Press the seams out.

5. Repeat Step 4 to add the top and bottom borders, this time measuring along the top, bottom, and center of the quilt (approximately 41″). Press the seams out.

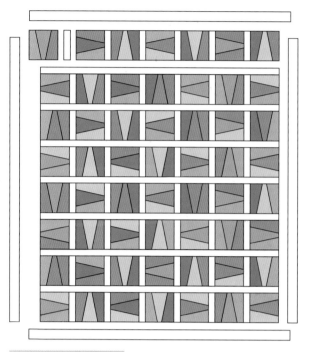

Figure 9—Quilt layout

Finishing

Refer to Finishing the Quilt (pages 16–23) for information on making the backing, quilting, and binding the quilt.

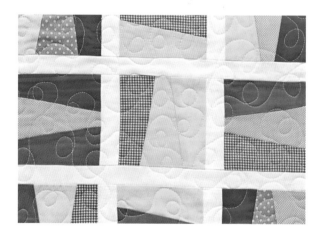

Sweets

Pieced by Allison Harris and quilted by Lindsay Szechenyi

This is one of the first quilts I made when I started quilting. At the time, I didn't know about strip piecing, so I cut out and sewed together all the little squares individually. Now I know a faster way, and I'm sharing it with you in this pattern. Even though I have given specific yardage requirements, I suggest adding extra 2½″ print strips for variety and to make the layout easier.

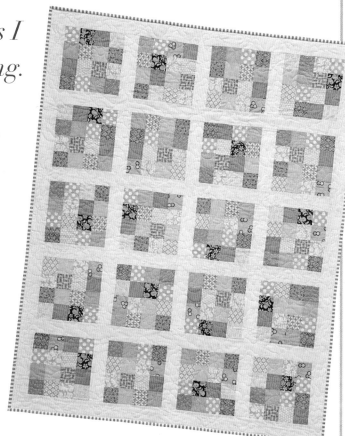

Quilt shown in a crib size

FINISHED BLOCK: 8″ × 8″

FINISHED QUILT • BABY: 32½″ × 42½″ • CRIB: 42½″ × 52½″ • TWIN: 62½″ × 82½″

Yardage is based on 42˝-wide fabric.

Size	Fabric	Yardage	Cutting	Subcut
Baby	Prints	¼ yard each of 4 fabrics*; *OR* 12 assorted strips 2½˝ × fabric width	3 strips 2½˝ × fabric width from each ¼ yard (12 total)	
	Neutral	¾ yard	2 strips 2½˝ × fabric width for vertical sashing	4 strips 2½˝ × 8½˝ from each strip (8 total)
			7 strips 2½˝ × fabric width for horizontal sashing and all borders	
	Backing	1½ yards		
	Binding	⅜ yard	4 strips 2½˝ × fabric width	
	Batting	37˝ × 47˝		

* For more variety and to make layout easier, add in extra 2½˝ × fabric-width strips.

Size	Fabric	Yardage	Cutting	Subcut
Crib	Prints	¼ yard each of 7 fabrics*; OR 20 strips 2½″ × fabric width	3 strips 2½″ × fabric width from each ¼ yard (20 total)	
	Neutral	1 yard	4 strips 2½″ × fabric width for vertical sashing	4 strips 2½″ × 8½″ from each strip (15 total)
			9 strips 2½″ × fabric width for horizontal sashing and all borders	
	Backing	2¾ yards		
	Binding	½ yard	6 strips 2½″ × fabric width	
	Batting	47″ × 57″		

* For more variety and to make layout easier, add in extra 2½″ × fabric-width strips.

Size	Fabric	Yardage	Cutting	Subcut
Twin	Prints	¼ yard each of 16 fabrics*; OR 48 strips 2½˝ × fabric width	3 strips 2½˝ × fabric width from each ¼ yard (48 total)	
	Neutral	2⅛ yards	10 strips 2½˝ × fabric width for vertical sashing	4 strips 2½˝ × 8½˝ from each strip (40 total)
			19 strips 2½˝ × fabric width for horizontal sashing and all borders	
	Backing	5 yards		
	Binding	⅝ yard	8 strips 2½˝ × fabric width	
	Batting	67˝ × 87˝		

For more variety and to make layout easier, add in extra 2½˝ × fabric-width strips.

Block Assembly

Note that all sewing is done right sides together with a ¼″ seam allowance.

1. Use the 2½″ strips as follows:

12 strips for the baby size

20 strips for the crib size

48 strips for the twin size

Sew the strips into sets of 4, using a different fabric order for each strip set (Figure 1). I recommend pressing open the strip set seams to make block assembly easier. Make 3 strip sets for the baby size, 5 strip sets for the crib size and 12 strip sets for the twin size.

2. Cut each strip set into 16 strips 2½″ × 8½″ (Figure 2).

3. Mix the 2½″ strips. Pin and sew 4 strips together (Figure 3). Press the seams open.

4. Make:

12 blocks for the baby size

20 blocks for the crib size

48 blocks for the twin size

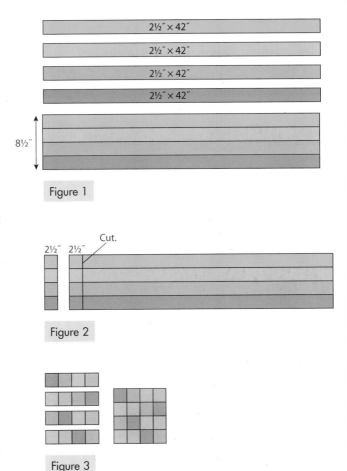

2½″ × 42″

2½″ × 42″

2½″ × 42″

2½″ × 42″

8½″

Figure 1

2½″ 2½″   Cut.

Figure 2

Figure 3

Quilt Top Assembly

1. Lay out the blocks as follows: (Figure 4):

4 rows of 3 blocks for the baby size

5 rows of 4 blocks for the crib size

8 rows of 6 blocks for the twin size

2. Place a neutral 2½″ × 8½″ strip vertically between each of the blocks in each row. Sew the blocks and strips together to make the rows. Press the seams toward the blocks.

3. Measure each row and take the average of the measurements. For the baby and crib size, mark that measurement with a pin along a 2½″ × fabric-width strip to be placed between each row. You'll need:

3 strips, approximately 28½″ for the baby size

4 strips, approximately 38½″ for the crib size

For the twin size, sew 11 neutral 2½″ × fabric-width strips together end to end. Press open. Measure the rows, take the average, and trim 7 neutral strips to that length from the long strip (approximately 58½″).

Pin and sew the horizontal sashing strip between the first 2 rows. Trim and press well toward the sashing. Continue pinning, sewing, and pressing the strips between each row to finish the quilt top.

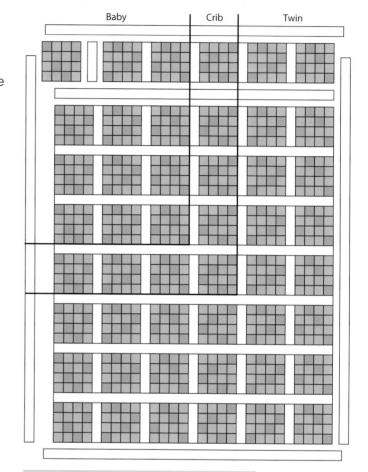

Figure 4—Quilt layout. All sizes have a border.

4. Refer to Adding Borders (page 14) to add the borders. For the baby quilt, measure and cut the border strips from the remaining neutral 2½˝ × fabric-width strips (approximately 38½˝ for the sides and 32½˝ for the top and bottom).

For the crib or twin size, sew the remaining neutral 2½˝ × fabric-width strips end to end and press the seams open. Measure the quilt top from top to bottom along the sides and in the center. Take the average of the measurements (approximately 48½˝ for the crib size and 78½˝ for the twin size). Mark that measurement with a pin along the strip length, sew the border strip to one side of the quilt, trim, and repeat with the other side. Press the seams out. Repeat this step with the top and bottom borders, except measure from side to side along the top, bottom, and center of the quilt (approximately 42½˝ for the crib size and 62½˝ for the twin size). Press the seams out.

Finishing

Refer to Finishing the Quilt (pages 16–23) for information on making the backing, quilting, and binding the quilt.

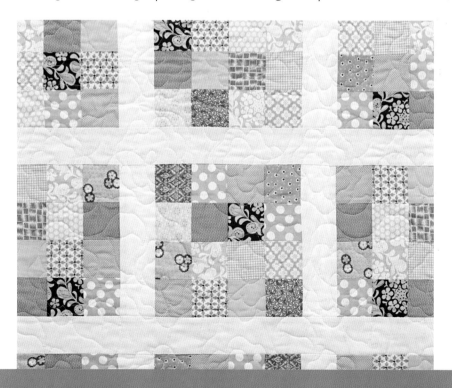

Resources

PRINT FABRICS

Many of the fabrics used may not be available anymore, but by visiting the manufacturer websites, you can view current or future collections.

Alexander Henry Fabrics
ahfabrics.com

Andover Fabrics
andoverfabrics.com

Birch Organic Fabric
birchfabrics.com

Free Spirit Fabrics
freespiritfabric.com

Michael Miller Fabrics
michaelmillerfabrics.com

Moda Fabrics
unitednotions.com

Riley Blake Designs
rileyblakedesigns.com

Robert Kaufman Fabrics
robertkaufman.com

SOLID FABRICS

Kona Cotton Solids
robertkaufman.com

Moda Bella Solids
unitednotions.com

LONGARM QUILTING SERVICES

Christina Lane
thesometimescrafter.com

Lindsay Szechenyi
eileenquilts.com

About the Author

Allison Harris is a country girl at heart who loves simple, clean designs and vibrant colors. She is a stay-at-home mom to three—Benjamin, Ryan, and Sophie. She graduated from college as a dental hygienist, but now spends her time raising her family, cleaning up Legos, cooking, sewing, and blogging. Allison calls the Seattle area home and hopefully always will.

ALLISON'S BLOG: cluckclucksew.com • PATTERNS: cluckclucksewpatterns.com